# Harmony
## and the Bhagavad-gita

*The talks of the Bhagavad-gita*
*are not for any particular person, society or community,*
*but they are for all.*

His Divine Grace A. C. Bhaktivedanta Swami Prabhupada

# Harmony
## and the Bhagavad-gita

Lessons from a Life-Changing Move to the Wilderness

Visakha

Other books by Visakha:

*Photomacrography: Art and Techniques*
*Our Most Dear Friend: Bhagavad-gita for Children*
*Bhagavad-gita: A Photographic Essay*

Quoted text from the Bhagavad-gita, Sri Isopanisad, Srimad-Bhagavatam, Chaitanya Charitamrita and Bhaktivedanta Swami Prabhupada courtesy of:

The Bhaktivedanta Book Trust International, Inc., www.Krishna.com. Used with permission.



*On the cover:* December in Sharanagati Village
*On the back:* Sharanagati Valley from Cornwall Mountain
*Insets:* Residents and guests of Sharanagati Village

*To*
*Bhaktivedanta*
*Swami*
*Prabhupada,*
*who kindly presented*
*the Bhagavad-gita*
*as it is.*

# Contents

# Introduction

In June of 1999 my family and I moved from our Los Angeles apartment to Sharanagati, a remote 1600-acre valley in British Columbia where a small band of semi-rugged, spiritually-minded individualists had settled. My mother-in-law said, "They'll last two years there – three at the most – before they move again." In the twenty-eight years since my husband and I have been married, we've moved every two to five years, so my mother-in-law wasn't being unduly pessimistic.

The Sharanagati community was isolated, off the grid, hours from a significant city, and functioned at its own sweet pace – a slow-motion crawl. Here we planned to start a new life, free of electric bills, fluorinated water, noise, traffic, bad air, billboards, crime and TV.

The home we rented, and then bought ten months later, was a small wooden house on a knoll overlooking grassland. In the distance, a mile-long lake shimmered through trees, flanked by fir- and pine-covered mountains. We were living inside a picture postcard. Our 5-year-old daughter was the twenty-second student in the valley's one-room schoolhouse, which accommodated grades Kindergarten to 12. We renovated our home, used a woodstove for heat, and an outhouse for nature's call. Our tap water was gravity-fed from a small aquifer on the mountain slope a quarter-mile away. Our electricity was from a solar panel. We grew vegetables and planted fruit trees. Except for our old Toyota Camry sedan and "3000" Honda generator (back-up power for overcast days), our self-sufficiency was nearly tangible.

Sharanagati, formidably enough, means "surrender" in Sanskrit. Here, among the rhythms of nature, near sincere fellow seekers, while confronting the wildness of our own mind, perhaps we could purify our lives. Perhaps those long winter nights and endless summer days would forge different people out of us: people closer to the earth, to simple faith, to contented, noncommercial, commodity-free lives. Perhaps observing Canadian loons and black bears while taking long walks in dense forests, working the soil with our hands, feeling glad about the things we grew and the miracles around us, we would begin to distinguish reality from illusion. Perhaps our new life, nourished by good cheer and harmony, could be our tiny contribution to the well-being of others. Surely, with less stress and more open sky, our epiphanies would reveal our essential identity and the purpose of existence.

What actually happened was quite different. Black bears ate our carrot crop and broke our apple trees to get our apples. Aphids attacked our berry bushes and ravished our Russian kale. Mice used almost mystic

powers to get into our sealed root cellar. A neighbor's nineteen-year-old son broke into and robbed our house. In January it was minus 30 degrees F. In July it topped 100. The winters were dreary, the summers mosquito-filled, and the autumns dry. In 2003, a forest fire burned 25,000 forested acres just north of us. At one point, drenched in terror, we saw flames shooting over the eastern ridge less than a mile away.

Through all of this, except the forest fire (which was too intense), I continued to read the renowned spiritual guidebook of the East, Bhagavad-gita, and to become more conscious of my incredible smallness, ignorance and uncertainties. I wondered about my purpose in living in Sharanagati and the purpose of living in the world generally; I wondered about country-style survival and about the urban cycle of continually making and spending money; I wondered about innocent and less than innocent diversions from the daily grind; I wondered about the relationship between values and happiness.

Gradually, my disparate experiences and reflections drew together under the canopy of harmony: the pleasing and diverse unity overarching all things and all beings. The saint Bhaktivedanta Swami Prabhupada, who translated and commented on the verses of Bhagavad-gita, once said, "Material or spiritual, everything is in harmony. That is God's law. Everything is in harmony." The simplicity and complexity of how this is so is for me the ecstatic mystery Bhagavad-gita explores. This, the true harvest of daily life in Sharanagati, is somewhat as intangible and indescribable as the tints of morning.

The three of us have lived in Sharanagati for many years now, but sadly my mother-in-law can't be surprised by the news of our perseverance in the wilderness for so long, as she passed away three years after we moved here. I think she would have liked the harmony in Sharanagati too, at least in the spring, summer and fall.

1

# Harmony Within

*In the beginning of the Bhagavad-gita, Krishna – God – will establish that living beings are not material: we are neither our body nor our mind nor our intellect. Thus who we think we are – all our bodily identifications according to gender, race, religion, social status, nationality, age, intelligence, qualities or abilities – is not who we truly are, but only our external and transient "dress." We, Krishna says, are spiritual beings. Until we entertain that dimension any attempt at inner happiness and harmony can be only superficial.*

**Now I am confused about my duty and have lost all composure because of miserly weakness. 2.7**

(Krishna's friend, Arjuna, speaking when confronted with a seemingly impossible choice)

## Disharmony

A half-mile from our Los Angeles apartment was a concrete-lined canal that fed into the ocean. A bike path ran alongside the canal, and two or three times a week I'd make the six-mile ride to the Pacific just to spend a few moments taking the salty air and the immensity of an unobstructed horizon deep inside me, giving me a small respite from the concrete-metal-glass "ocean" that I lived in. One afternoon, on my way from our apartment to the bike path, I saw the road in front of the neighborhood police station torn up and patches of dark quiet soil between its broken slabs. My first thought was, "Wow, there's earth under the road!" The next moment, when I thought about it, my sealed heart sighed for our city days to end. Later, I found that my husband John also felt our lives had become somewhat dull and suffocating, that we'd lost some invisible yet vital rootedness and breadth. A road repair had sparked a dilemma: where to move? – a dilemma of minor angst, but angst nonetheless.

Bhagavad-gita – the five-thousand-year-old "Song of God" and arguably one of the oldest and most beautiful spiritual teachings in existence – begins with a dilemma. In the above verse from the second chapter, the hero Arjuna, torn between duty and desire, between logic and emotion, between two correct yet incorrect courses of action, faces a dilemma just as my husband and I did and all of us will at one point of time or other. Arjuna's question is, "Shall I fight my kinsmen or not?"

Ours could be, "Where should we live?" "What should I study?" "How should I earn a living?" "Whom should I marry?" And sometimes the bigger questions: "Who am I?" "Why am I here?" Dilemma is an integral part of the human condition.

Over the course of its eighteen chapters, Bhagavad-gita reveals why we make the choices we do and how, for better or worse, those choices affect us. Due to poor choices I was stressed and deeply troubled. I wanted a

meaningful life, but poor choices had left me anguished with the thought that perhaps I didn't have one. Perhaps I'd accepted a senseless life simply because so many others had. I was as debilitated by confusion as Arjuna was. I could have turned to excesses and obsessions with drugs, affairs, work, the internet, food, investments, shopping sprees, useless possessions and empty politics. But I hungered for something else. I was no longer satisfied with the superficial identity and purpose others had pressed on me; I no longer wanted to act in a way that contradicted who I was. It was time for my family and me to live in a place where the air was more breathable, birds' songs more audible, and our roots could reach meaningfulness. But where?

"Forget about moving to Sharanagati," my husband, a freelance video editor, said one morning.

"Why?" I said, suddenly realizing how much I wanted to move there.

"It's way too cold in the winter and it's too isolated. There's no way we'll be happy there."

"Maybe. But there's a house there just the right size for us that we can rent with the option to buy. The owner is offering us a deal," I said. "Plus, there's a school in Sharanagati that I think will be great for Priya."

John wavered.

Dilemma was prodding John and me to understand our real business in this world and saving us from the falsity of feigned joviality in a trivial existence and the hollowness of a workaholic life. Dilemma was allowing us to find insights far beyond the intellect to live by. In Arjuna's case, he knew that wealth, education and talent would not drive away his confusion. He needed to resolve his disharmony by hearing from Krishna. Therefore he said, "Krishna, please instruct me." Any other solution would not have saved him.

Perhaps my family and I could also gradually triumph over superficiality and penetrate the mystery of harmony. In this life-clarifying passage, Bhagavad-gita would be our guidebook; for our seismic shift that singular book was with us.

*I know of no more encouraging fact than the unquestionable ability of man to elevate his life by conscious endeavor.*

— Henry David Thoreau

*I owed a magnificent day to the Bhagavad-gita. It was the first of books; it was as if an empire spoke to us, nothing small or unworthy, but large, serene, consistent, the voice of an old intelligence which in another age and climate had pondered and thus disposed of the same questions which exercise us.*

— Ralph Waldo Emerson

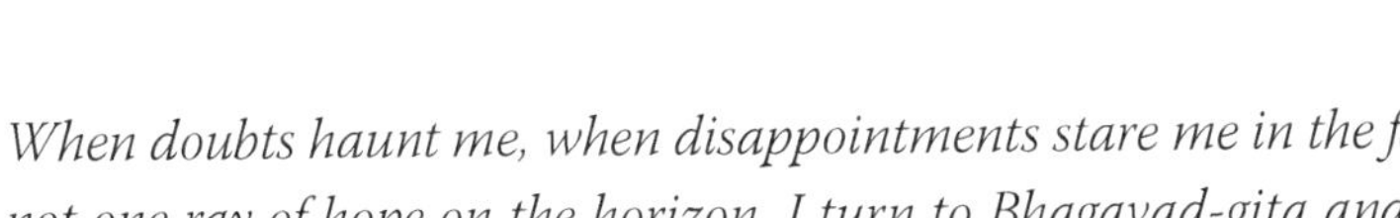

*When doubts haunt me, when disappointments stare me in the face and I see not one ray of hope on the horizon, I turn to Bhagavad-gita and find a verse to comfort me; and I immediately begin to smile in the midst of overwhelming sorrow. Those who meditate on the Gita will derive fresh joy and new meanings from it every day.*

— Mohandas (Mahatma) Gandhi

**The soul [*jivatma*] is unborn, eternal, immortal and primeval. It does not die when the body dies. 2.20**

## Jivatma

I first heard about *jivatma* – the soul – in 1971 during my maiden overseas trip. I was reuniting with my then-boyfriend (later husband) John in India, and to me, a born and bred atheist, *jivatma* was a quaint irrelevant idea.

An idea, however, can be like a seed: it can germinate.

As a wizened juniper sapling clings to a weathered cliff so, despite the harsh winds of skepticism and flurries of distractions, the idea of *jivatma* embedded itself in my heart and grew into wispy "what ifs." What if the body contained an infinitesimal spiritual particle – the soul – that is the antithesis of the body, a particle that wasn't born and doesn't die, that was indestructible and everlasting?

What if the soul is the body's source of life and consciousness as the sun is the universe's source of heat and light? What if life doesn't come from a perishable, chance combination of material elements? As a photojournalist exploring Mumbai, these musings coaxed me from blaring car horns and teeming streets to some curious transcendent possibility. The mythical, irrelevant idea of *jivatma* began delicately to undermine what had been for me a lifetime of hidden hopelessness:

What's the point of life, of peace, of accomplishment – of anything – if everything is a fleeting combination of elements? Why distinguish evil from honorable, orderliness from mess? And why work so hard?

More than a consoling theory to save me from confusion and gloom, without my intending it the plausibility of *jivatma* gradually changed my perception. Early one morning, before Mumbai's bustle began, I watched a bullock cart lumber up to one of the city's most popular sweet shops. Immediately, four robust men from the shop began unloading the cart's six 20-gallon aluminum containers of fresh milk. One after the other they emptied the containers, the milk flowing like a waterfall in springtime, into six huge black iron woks that already had high flames under them. Skinny boys, holding long brass rods with wide flat ends, began stirring the milk. Meanwhile, a woman in tatters with three small children in equally threadbare clothes walked up. She tipped over each one of the empty and now relatively light containers, allowing the tiny

bit of milk left in them to trickle into an earthen jug one of her children held. By the time she had tipped over all six containers her jug was full of fresh milk. The sweet shop workers ignored her, giving me the impression it was a regular routine. This woman carried herself with such dignity and cheer, was so conscientious of her task and loving with her children, that despite her humble activity I found myself considering her not as a poor person or a woman or an Indian, but as an individual animated by a noble, shining, divine spark. The soul's presence was becoming conceivable.

In Bhagavad-gita Krishna claims that the core of Arjuna's dilemma, and so also the core of mine – and everyone else's – is that we've forgotten who we are. We're a soul (*jivatma* in Sanskrit) Krishna says, that resides in the temporary body. The soul is subtler than the senses and so cannot be seen, touched or tasted. It is beyond intelligence, which acquires and analyzes information, and beyond the mind, which wants to exploit what the senses perceive. The soul is beyond time and space. Its presence in the heart animates the body and its absence reveals the body's true nature: a corpse.

So, decades after Mumbai, pushed by the sickening endless stress of Los Angeles life and pulled by a spiritual call, John and I put aside our fear of amenities lost to raw simplicity, packed all we owned into boxes, helped Priya mark each box with its contents, put them in a rented truck and headed north. Trepidation melded with hope and joy as a five-year-old and two graying pioneers with young hearts waiting to be unboxed drove off, ready to be all they were meant to be, ready to renew their love for life and for each other and to explore their own lovability; ready to be themselves – *jivatmas*.

As we passed the modern clutter of human attempts for happiness in the form of cavernous malls, places for fast and thoughtless food, rows of office buildings, alluring yet dizzying shopping centers, I considered that simply by observing myself I could experience *jivatma's* presence: how I always sought happiness and *jivatma* is always happy; how I didn't want to die and *jivatma* is eternal; how I yearned for meaning and understanding and *jivatma* is purposeful and knowledgeable; how I was convinced of my importance and *jivatma* is innately important; how, despite my age, I felt young and *jivatma* is youthful.

It didn't end there. I thought of how at odd moments, while being caressed by the ocean breeze, I could feel that I was self-satisfied and loved to give of myself; *jivatma* is fulfilled and flourishes through selfless service. I really didn't need to compare myself to others or to be special and popular.

In all the many years between Mumbai and Los Angeles the tenacious idea of *jivatma* remained rooted in the rocky outpost of my heart. And now part of me wanted to try to be who I am, try to untie the knot of ignorance that made me misidentify myself with my mind and body. Maybe I was an alien in the city hubbub because I was alien to my actual self; maybe it was *jivatma* who cried from my heart, "Go beyond the surface of existence!" *Jivatma*, my mysterious inner voice, knows that the body and mind it animates have a refined importance and purpose. *Jivatma* is dedicated to that purpose.

That tiny spiritual particle rejects the way I misuse my body, my mind and a society that supports such misuse. But to be *jivatma*-conscious I felt I needed a *jivatma*-compatible place. Fortunately, John wanted the same for himself, and we both wanted it for Priya.

Sharanagati was austere and remote, but it was perhaps the only place where my family and I could learn that sacredness wasn't complicated and impossible. I am, and we all are, already sacred. To realize our sacredness, some of us – like my family and I – needed to live in a place more sanctified than a city, a natural place with people who lived lightly on this earth, people filled with wonder and love, yearning and gratitude.

*What you are looking for is what is looking.*

— St. Francis of Assisi

*Within us lies something incomparably more precious than what we see outside ourselves.*

— St. Teresa of Avila

*She had always known that her body was just a shell she lived in, but it occurred to her now that her mind was yet another shell – in which case, who was "she"?*

— Anne Tyler

*I stood up and put my hand on the tombstone and saw it for what it is, only a place where mortal remains lay. The body was there, to be sure, but it was only a coat that had been laid off because the wearer needed it no longer. But she, that gloriously lovely spirit, she was not there.*

— Norman Vincent Peale

**In this world, those who are on this path are resolute in purpose, and their aim is one. 2.41**

## Resolution

Three days and 1500 miles after leaving Los Angeles, John, Priya and I pulled into the driveway of our small, chocolate-colored, wood-sided Sharanagati rental. Until this moment the house had been a sight unseen, and as I peered through the windshield at its small windows and noted the path an animal had made burrowing through the straw bale insulation in its crawl space, misgivings crept over me. What kind of place was this? Stiff from sitting, I stepped down from the truck into Sharanagati's silent, spacious beauty. Its unsullied air, its endless sun-soaked hillocks and draws, its huge brilliant blue sky brought me face to face with some profound yet warm reality that welcomed and embraced me.

I was elated. John, Priya and I had actually done it. We'd broken free. We'd made a scary, revolutionary move not based on our work, on what others expected of us – and certainly not on the climate or on our convenience! – but on what was best for us as a family and as individuals. Even the still unknown condition of our rental didn't dampen my spirits. John and I figured our monthly expenses here would be a third of what they'd been in Los Angeles.

A couple of days later, just after we'd emptied our last moving box, I was on the southern slope next to our new home, pulling weeds and shifting rocks to make space for a garden. It was a torrid and windless

June afternoon, and when I paused under the shade of a large fir, I became aware of a layer of activity at ground level – black ants; black-and-red ants that, I discovered, gave a wicked bite; small, medium and large ants. They walked hurriedly for a few inches and hesitated, sometimes consulting briefly with ants going the other way, slightly altered their course and rushed on. Soon I'd uncovered six large ant colonies under different rocks, each highly populated and furiously busy. Several contained about a hundred large, whitish, well-organized oval eggs that looked like rows of puffed rice. Every ant was acting in its specific function, with some clear and highly motivated intent. Apparently each ant was never discouraged and was rarely confused, even when its home was disturbed and the activity around it frenzied. By their nature the ants were determined, disciplined and harmonious.

I, however, was not an ant. Although I appreciated their resolute determination and cooperativeness, unlike them I didn't act simply out of instinct but had choices: I could choose to battle the ants or to ignore them. Although ant bites discouraged Priya from gardening, I could choose to be conscious of the higher self and to act according to its promptings, or to ignore the inner voice – the soul's voice – that wanted more than an ant-free garden. That voice wanted to be free from slaving to wants; it cried for something beyond getting educated, making a living, raising a family and leaving a good name for posterity. It insisted, "Life is more than a perpetual war against various troubles and miseries. It's meant for more than eating, sleeping, sexual satisfaction, work and recreation."

Bhagavad-gita unequivocally informed me that I was meant to function as *jivatma* – that is, to participate in the spiritual dimension of life. To do this was another kind of struggle as I, *jivatma*, transformed the theory of *jivatma* into practice. But I am an ordinary person, not a saint. Would this work? In these first weeks, the novelty of plowing the earth and the luxury of silence and open space made Sharanagati life a delight. But as weeks became months, years and decades, would I become robotic instead of resolute? Would this new life become as mindless as my old one?

Maybe, by following Bhagavad-gita's straightforward guidance, in our country setting my family and I, whatever our shortcomings, could live as *jivatmas*. The bedrock of our attempt would be resolution – our ongoing decision to defy our own contrary moods and doubts while trying to make the best choices, big and small, in the present moment. My husband and I could easily lose our focus and return to Los Angeles, but for our own good and because it was the best place we knew of for our daughter, we didn't make that choice. We stayed. In Sharanagati, swaddled by nature, we felt the chastity of our ant-like resolution would take even a grain of faith seriously and suspend unbelief; the mystery of resolution would allow us to trust the intangible, knowing that external events did not and never would possess ultimate power over us.

When I'm on my knees by myself – in my garden or my bedroom or a temple – through resolution I would take responsibility for my life, subordinate my feelings to my values, and risk replacing my old patterns of thought with fresh ones offered in the Gita. Through spiritual resolution I'd act for the good of *jivatma* and, with simple sincerity, avoid diversion and dryness.

So, "resolute" meant to keep focused, to tolerate troubles (including mosquitoes and children's messes), to be flexible before challenges, to discriminate between what to and what not to do and to learn from mistakes. After trying eco-friendly but ineffective ant deterrents, I avoided admitting defeat by ignoring the ants, only to discover that black bears enjoyed turning over our garden rocks to find and lap up colonies of them. Bears checked the ant population, and all I had to do was replace bear-turned rocks. (These bears were people-shy so we didn't have to fear them. In fact, we hardly even saw them.) If I could remain clear and resolute, at least some problems would work themselves out.

"Irresolute" means discouraged by my dullness, upset by difficulty and neglectful of *jivatma*, I'd live a humdrum life feeling like lost luggage, vulnerable to changing fortunes and others' opinions, with a blind hope in future happiness. Engrossed in work or using the many distractions society offers, I'd avoid the frightening experience of being alone and feeling the emptiness and futility of an existence captured only by externals.

The most important decision in my life fell to me: to accept my role, fulfill my duties and, at the same time, become aware of my identity and purpose. From the strength of resolution I could approach the choices and events in my life consciously, whether I was in the city, the country or in between. But for now, John, Priya and I were glad to be in the country. A month after we arrived in Sharanagati, Priya and I were planting our third pear tree when a plane flew high overhead, leaving a sky-long trail of white exhaust. Astonished, Priya looked up and said, "What is that?" with a tone that made me also wonder why it was necessary for a great, noisy metal contraption to mar the boundless pure blue yonder.

Ants were still busy at our feet, but there were less of them.

*Lose this day loitering – 'twill be the same story*
*To-morrow – and the next more dilatory;*
*For indecision brings its own delays,*
*And days are lost lamenting o'er lost days.*
*Are you in earnest? Seize this very minute!*
*Boldness has genius, power and magic in it.*
*Only engage, and then the mind grows heated;*
*Begin it, and the work will be completed.*

— Johann Wolfgang von Goethe

*A strong will is the best asset that a human being can possess, not because it guarantees success or goodness, but because a weak will pretty much guarantees failure.*

— M. Scott Peck

*With a new awareness, both painful and humorous, I begin to understand why the saints were rarely married women. I am convinced it has nothing inherently to do, as I once supposed, with chastity or children. It has to do primarily with distractions ... I want a singleness of eye, a purity of intention ... I want, in fact – to borrow from the language of the saints – to live "in grace" as much of the time as possible.*

— Ann Morrow Lindbergh

**The minds of those who are too attached to sense enjoyment and material opulence are bewildered. 2.44**

## Character

Near our new home was a crowded forest of skinny fir trees with crowns that stretched high up to reach air and light. While walking along the dirt road that cut through that forest, it occurred to me that our Sharanagati life was about learning to reach past inner darkness; it was about accessing the natural light of good character. While disharmony and resolution could lead to knowledge of *jivatma*, good character – my finer nature – was the sunlight of *jivatma* piercing my heart's density. Good character, the intrinsic spiritual rays that pervade my being, could give me the awareness and strength to dispute the dictates of my senses and mind. It was due to character that ethics and even spiritual discipline could become a surprisingly agreeable expression of my own will!

Each *jivatma*, each individual, is of character and is a character, a distinctive person. Since we had so few neighbors in our forest-encircled valley the importance and qualities of each of them seemed both magnified and sometimes magnificent. By and large our neighbors were like wildflowers not plucked and plunked in a vase to wilt, as I had been wilting in Los Angeles, but wildflowers that displayed their radiant beauty as they bobbed in the breeze, the glory of each heightened by the lush meadow around it. Nature's boundless beauty was enhancing my estimation of the people it enclosed.

While I was elbow-deep in garden earth, my closest neighbor to the south (a quarter-mile away), wiry and energetic Gisele, a French Canadian, stopped by holding a tray of food and said with a smile, "All your work will make you hungry, so I brought you some salad, soup and homemade bread – and I'm happy to see you love to garden! I do too."

Later, Yamuna Devi, a perceptive and quick-witted friend whom I'd known since my time in India in the '70s and who was now my closest neighbor to the north (also a quarter-mile away), laughed when she saw me flicking biting ants off my pants. "I would've told you more about the trials of Sharanagati life, but you really needed to experience them for yourself," she said, and as we sat together on my newly-placed garden rocks, she offered Sharanagati survival tips.

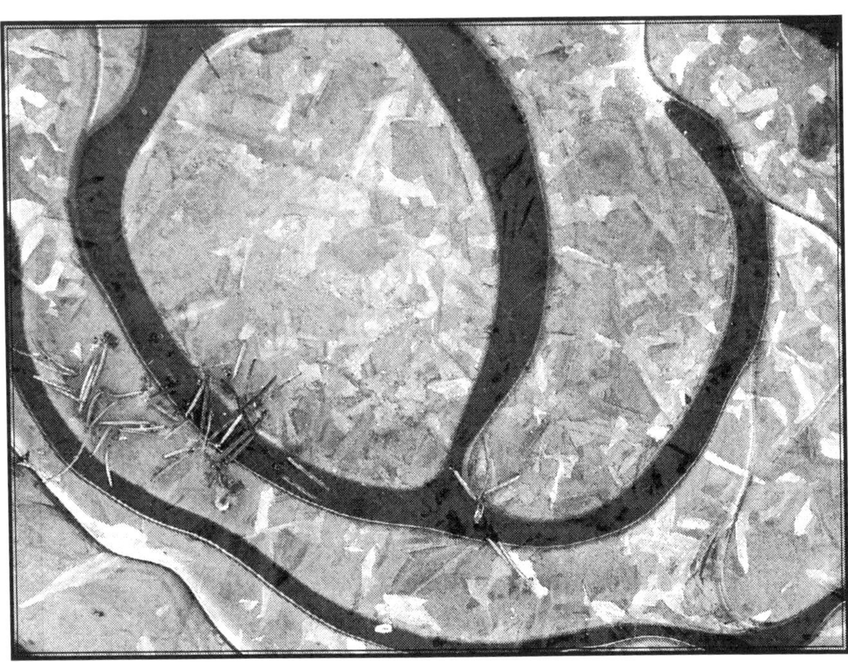

In Los Angeles I'd hardly known even one of our neighbors, who were just a few feet away, but here I got to know them all. The former Vancouver taxi-driver neighbor was easy-going, funny and competent in legal matters. The Italian carpenter was ever generous, helpful and an analyzer of personalities and motivations. The American soap-maker was thoughtful, quiet, responsible and lighthearted, and often offered a contrary yet valid point of view. But it wasn't all cheery, neighbor-wise. One old man proved unpredictably touchy, even grouchy. A couple of housewives were critical and condescending, another, an incessant talker. One neighbor was a maverick, another needy; one was meticulously clean, another overly lax, and another ever restless. Even so, to varying degrees every one of them had accepted some discipline to help themselves become free of the mind's whimsical dictates and were striving for the sublime, however long it would take to attain. Most prayed to never compromise their spiritual goal, and all warmly welcomed my family and me into their midst.

Without resolution and character my life would become chaotic and shattered. With them, clarity replaced confusion just as sunlight enveloped me whenever I moved toward it. While I basked in the qualities of many of my neighbors, I was challenged to go beyond others' quirks. Perhaps it was time for me to overlook the petty tangles individuality created and instead accept that a person's character was the result of many factors of which I was unaware. Instead of quirks, perhaps I could discover common interests and interesting differences between me and my neighbors. Perhaps, by stretching past the dense brambles of my own fixed impressions, I could finally grow up here in Sharanagati.

*But all the things that God would have us do are hard for us to do – remember that – and hence, he oftener commands us than endeavors to persuade. And if we obey God, we must disobey ourselves; and it is in this disobeying ourselves, wherein the hardness of obeying God consists.*

— Herman Melville *(Moby Dick)*

*Doing our own will is usually what harms us.*

— St. Teresa of Avila *(Interior Castle)*

*There is a kind of "wild card" within each of us, a well of courage and creativity we don't even know is in there until we learn how to tap into it through spiritual disciplines.*

— Carol Lee Flinders

**Abandon all attachment to success or failure. Such equanimity is called yoga. 2.48**

## Letting Go

The vistas of almost identical clouds with flat gray-blue undersides, the soaring hawks and lowing cows, the garden's vigorous green peas, the wars between plants and bugs, the giggles and squabbles of the girls, our friends with their different gifts and worries, the Sharanagati summer that lasts forever and then vanishes as the waving hills turn from verdant to amber – these make up the pulse of our new life. Letting go means to accept and give all I can to this life while remembering that one day I'll have to leave everything behind. Although I think in terms of my house, my land, my family, my friends, in a very real sense nothing is mine. If anything was really mine I wouldn't have to leave it behind when I passed away.

Letting go – detachment – is not indifference or inactivity; instead it means I take complete responsibility for what I'm doing, knowing that the success or failure of my action will follow in a manner often unforeseen and unforeseeable. Character endows clarity in what to do while detachment concentrates on the activity instead of the results. I put compost in our garden, I plant a bed of carrots, I weed and water daily for months, and then one crisp September morning I'm startled to find one carrot left in the whole bed. Overnight a bear had dug up and eaten the rest. I'm flabbergasted.

Attachment makes me fantasize that I can control the result of my efforts and binds me anxiously to success, which in fact is unpredictable. Detachment frees me of the fantasy of control over the outcome and also makes me ever so slightly more neutral when I view the lone carrot left after months of labor. As I accept that many things are beyond my domination, I can detect hidden balances, delights and even humor in nature's ways. In early August the next year, a neighbor came by and filled my biggest kitchen bowl with delectable baby carrots that he'd thinned from his garden.

"Bears don't eat your carrots?" I asked, incredulous.

"Nope," he said. "I plant them early and harvest them before the bears get to them. Bears are notoriously ravenous just before they hibernate in the fall."

My harvest of one carrot out of a whole crop was a Sharanagati lesson in detachment, freely offered to immunize me from the disappointment that comes from attachment to results and also to teach me the necessity of knowledge, which in this case meant timing. Yet I still tend to plant crops bears don't favor – Swiss chard, beets, zucchini, herbs – and leave carrots to more intrepid gardeners.

Character will let me act with valor, while detachment will let me accept whatever comes. This is karma-yoga, responsible action without strings attached, which brings me to the stark reality that nothing is mine other than my consecrated duty. Through karma-yoga I approach

God by dedicating my honest work and its fruits to Him. And yes, that cool September morning I did thank God for my one carrot – but with a grimace.

By gradually detaching me from the pleasant or unpleasant results of my efforts, karma-yoga makes my outer activity, which is impermanent, subservient to my lofty goal, which has lasting value. Krishna tells Arjuna:

> Without being attached to the fruits of activities, one should act as a matter of duty, for by working without attachment one attains the Supreme.
>
> — Bhagavad-gita 3.19

To give everything and then to let go completely is possible when I stitch the quilt of my life with spiritual intent. Detachment lets me fix my attention on the immediate moment, allows the future to take care of itself and relies on the past for the wisdom of knowing what to do right now. This positive and full absorption in the present is freedom. Detachment lets me harvest happiness despite the many and diverse one-carrot surprises of Sharanagati life.

*Often, we think of detachment as the magic ticket that will allow us to bypass the spills and chills of loving others. It may more accurately be the ticket that allows us to accept the spills and chills of loving.*

— Julia Cameron

*There is no charm here that shall make us hesitate to withdraw from this world, but our life in this world is valuable. With this life we can acquire a higher aspiration. We can have the chance of acquiring the goal from this plane. This human life is so valuable that with it we can take the path of the highest divine conception.*

— B. R. Sridhar Swami

**We may restrict ourselves from sense enjoyment, though the taste for sense objects remains. But, ceasing such engagements by experiencing a higher taste, we are fixed in consciousness. 2.59**

## Satisfaction

By my nature I, a *jivatma*, am satisfied. In my first few Sharanagati months I discovered how this innate satisfaction didn't arise from accumulating tangibles, but swelled up unheralded when I was gratified by whatever I already had.

I didn't really have much. My family and I were living in a small home, eating simple food, doing ordinary things. Yet I was opulent: I was wholeheartedly accepting my circumstances and self as they were and was content with my activity of the moment. I wasn't measuring success by the size of my salary, but was beginning to gauge it by how I allowed the wheel of my motivation to revolve around the axle of spirit.

> Even the entirety of whatever there may be within the three worlds to satisfy one's senses cannot satisfy a person whose senses are uncontrolled.... One should be satisfied with whatever he achieves by his previous destiny, for discontent can never bring happiness.
>
> — Srimad-Bhagavatam 8.19.21, 24

I loved my life in Sharanagati. Everything I needed was here. But at times discontent reigned: I should do more and have more and be more. After all, in my youth I was set to become a world-class photographer; now I was just a housewife-mother-gardener-writer. Modern society's allure is a phantom that pervades the planet, saying: unless you achieve and are important and have things you should not be satisfied. So how could I be satisfied with so little distinction and so few assets? Shouldn't I find work with a nationally syndicated agency? Shouldn't I be wealthier? And above all, don't I need Apple's latest gizmo?

Bhagavad-gita's message is that I will be truly satisfied when I include God in my life:

> Whatever you do, whatever you eat, whatever you offer or give away, and whatever austerities you perform – do that as an offering to Me.
>
> — Bhagavad-gita 9.27, Krishna speaking

In this present moment, right now, it is devotion to the task at hand that gives work meaning and purpose in terms of our identity as *jivatma*

– a soul. Even in the humble acts of pulling blood-red beets from the ground, cleaning, cutting and cooking them, thanking God for kindly providing this bounty for us, and then sharing my homemade borscht with family and neighbors, some long-buried feelings of rightness and completeness organically emerge, washing over and nurturing me. I never knew that happiness could be so simple and so integral to life.

In an open area a short walk from our home, alongside a winding and aspen-covered creek, are the remains of several frontier log cabins that

pioneers labored to build more than a hundred and fifty years ago. The roofs have fallen in and trees grow inside them, but their eighteen-inch-thick walls are still strong and could remain standing another hundred years. These men and women struggled and died without special recognition or greatness. The gravesite of one of them is hidden among some firs on a hilltop not far from the cabins. I have no way of knowing if they were satisfied with their rugged life but, when pines are poking through the floorboards in my home, may my descendents honestly be able to say, "Yes, she found satisfaction."

*What do I need to be happy? God has given me the ability to be happy in my own situation simply by accepting what is present before me and doing the best I can with it. Can I not be content with this personal happiness? Do I need to get someone else's approval before my guilt and anxiety cease? Do I need to measure my happiness against my neighbor's (who may be across the planet) to be certain that I am indeed happy? Can happiness that's free, available to anyone anywhere and at any time, private and personal, be genuine? We are quite capable of being happy in the life He has provided for us, in which we can contentedly make our own way, helped by His grace. We are ashamed to do so. For we need one thing more than happiness: we need approval. And the need for approval destroys our capacity for happiness.*

— Thomas Merton

*For spiritual advancement, one should be materially satisfied, for if one is not materially satisfied, his greed for material development will result in frustration of his spiritual advancement. There are two things that nullify all good qualities. One is poverty. The other is greed. The adjustment is that one should not be poverty stricken, but one must try to be fully satisfied with the bare necessities of life and not be greedy.*

— Bhaktivedanta Swami Prabhupada

**One who restrains the senses but whose mind dwells on sense objects is certainly deluded and is called a pretender. 3.6**

## Cheating

I'd gone from disharmony to knowledge of *jivatma* – the soul – and had learned of the tenacity, moral firmness and the inner grounding that a self-aware *jivatma* reveals. Sometimes, however, when I forgot all that, my declared and actual aims parted ways and I wanted to cheat, to get something without earning it, to pretend I was less worldly than I actually was, to become rich and famous as an eco-friendly forest saint. Cheating, a fissure in life's foundation, would unceremoniously toss me back into the lap of disharmony.

> If one is not factually detached from material activities but still proclaims himself advanced in devotional service, he is cheating. No one will be happy to see such behavior.
>
> — Bhaktivedanta Swami Prabhupada

Hypocrisy skulks next to me, intrinsic to the materialistic mind, and I could not afford to ignore it as it covets wealth or followers while pretending to be virtuous and spiritual. When I felt some shortcoming within myself, when ambition, pleasure, or my need for security pushed me to cheat, it meant that I was ignoring my own ever-worthy presence: a sweet, discrete *jivatma*. Although in the past my heart has been pierced and my faith vandalized by cheaters – unkind relatives, false friends, misleading teachers, conniving politicians – the pain I felt when I was cheated could not match the anguish I'd eventually feel if I cheated. Being cheated is often beyond my control, but if I cheated it meant I'd sacrificed my self for self-aggrandizement, that ultimately I was untrue to myself.

If I pretend this book has "the truth" but actually write it only to make a buck or a reputation, I'm cheating. The American educator and writer Will Durant went so far as to say, "All writing for publication is exhibitionism." But I have the urge to write; what to do?

In Bhagavad-gita Krishna responds to the accusations of exhibitionism and pretension by telling Arjuna,

> Even knowledgeable people act according to their own nature, for all people follow the nature they have acquired. What can repression accomplish?
>
> — Bhagavad-gita 3.33

In other words, I'm not to neglect my inclination to write but I'm to write with a sacred objective, entering into the inner meaning of experiences that I habitually gloss over and thinking deeply about purpose and attitude. Writing this book was clarifying and uplifting; it was a chance to check my real against my declared aims, a chance to try to purge myself of the cheating tendency, a chance to come closer to harmony. And it was a great way to pass those long Sharanagati winters.

Happily I show guests the well-shaped Norda apple tree I planted in our front yard two years after we moved here; but that tree's vitality is hidden in its roots; the source of its strength has nothing to do with me. In the same way, although I may parade some externals of good fortune, God is the source of that good fortune, and He knows the strength and course of my roots, my interior life. If the externals – the branches and leaves – are separated from those roots they're fit only for kindling. Similarly, my life will eventually dry up if false motives prevail over genuine ones, if I finagle.

Like everyone, I hunger for integrity. I don't have to passively resign myself to the cheating that will eventually decay every great and small thing I do. In resisting cheating I can see that the neediness that drives me to it is the false burden of trying to be more than exactly who I am. That burden dissipates as soon as the deeply hidden *jivatma* consents to God's design and is satisfied with its moment in history and its obscure task in it. When I even tentatively seek inspiration from Bhagavad-gita I feel a renaissance of hope and a bond with providence. In the final issue, what can I be proud of? What can I take credit for? Everything is coming from God, including whatever abilities I may have. The credit rightfully goes to Him.

If I, a former ardent atheist, can feel the tiniest presence of divinity, then anyone can. This feeling evokes a satisfying fit between my inner and outer world: a harmony that allows me to immerse myself and flourish in my own niche while living a simple life that's mostly free of cheating. Cheating, it seems, is far more obvious and obnoxious when it shows up in natural surroundings. The chipmunks that scurry around our home are free of it.

*If we compromise our integrity for the thrills of this world we will suffer in the future.*

— Radhanatha Swami

*Truth and sincerity have a certain distinguishing native luster about them, which cannot be perfectly counterfeited; they are like fire and flame, which cannot be painted.*

— Benjamin Franklin

*These are my principles. If you don't like them, I've got others.*

— Groucho Marx

**The spirit soul bewildered by a lack of knowledge thinks itself the doer of activities. 3.27**

## It's Under Control

One morning in early October I was scraping ice off our windshield before driving Priya to school and thinking nervously, "If this is October weather, January will be arctic; maybe John was right – it was a mistake to move to Sharanagati ... But it's too late to turn back now. We'll have to face winter's cruelties." Clearly, I couldn't control the dropping temperatures, but I could learn how to best use the little controlling power I did have.

Because I, a *jivatma*, am an intrinsic part of God I have a finite degree of God's infinite qualities. God is joyful and innately I am too. God is the fully independent supreme controller and I have minute independence and control. With impeccable discernment God acts and then takes full responsibility for everything He does, and I am meant to do likewise.

As *jivatma* I have the wisdom to discern what is to be done and what is not to be done, act accordingly and accept responsibility for what I do. My sense of discernment, however, depends on my knowledge and my confidence in that knowledge. In the opening chapters of Bhagavad-gita Arjuna himself lacked knowledge and confidence, as when he said to Krishna:

> Although these enemy soldiers, their hearts overtaken by greed, see no fault in killing their family or quarreling with friends, why should we, who can see the crime in destroying a family, engage in such acts of sin?
>
> — Bhagavad-gita 1.37–38

Understandably, Arjuna doesn't want to fight his family members. Yet, on a deeper level, Arjuna's lack of knowledge made him misunderstand his duty, act irresponsibly and become miserable. This was clear moments later:

> Arjuna, having thus spoken, cast aside his bow and arrows and sat down on the chariot, his mind overwhelmed with grief.
>
> — Bhagavad-gita 1.46

Often I may think I'm discerning when in reality my discernment is topsy-turvy, and the result, like Arjuna's, is misery.

By recognizing my smallness and my dependence on God, gradually I can learn to discern with accuracy, act with discretion and take responsibility for what I do. My progress is in the art of proper choices, actions and acceptance and, as in Arjuna's case, the best choice may not be obvious.

Discernment pokes its nose into all of life's aspects: in how John and I earn and spend money, in how much time John and I spend with Priya and in what we do in that time, in what books we read and movies we watch, in what we choose to say and not to say, in our priorities, in the company we keep.

And discernment can shift over time, as we found out community-wise in Sharanagati. Twenty-five years after he'd moved to Sharanagati one old-timer found that his values had so altered that instead of his former simple, healthy and celibate lifestyle, he now wanted intoxication and sex. Our other neighbors, along with John and I, were in consternation: we didn't move to Sharanagati so our kids would grow up around people who were high and licentious. Since Priya was old enough now to understand, I explained to her how I felt about pot-smoking.

"We don't want you to be around people who smoke pot."

"What's wrong with pot?" she said.

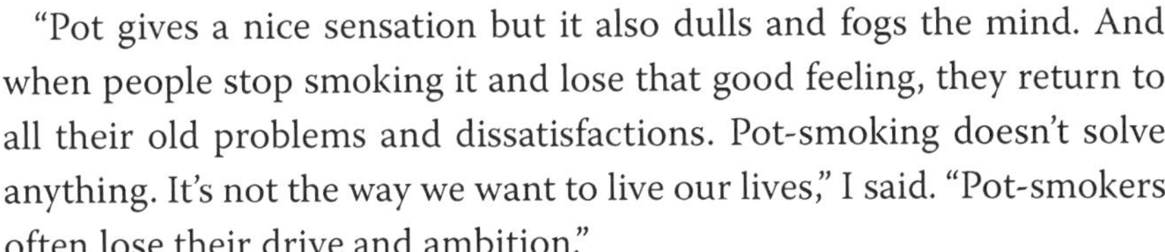

"Pot gives a nice sensation but it also dulls and fogs the mind. And when people stop smoking it and lose that good feeling, they return to all their old problems and dissatisfactions. Pot-smoking doesn't solve anything. It's not the way we want to live our lives," I said. "Pot-smokers often lose their drive and ambition."

"Hmm," she said, expecting more.

"If we're just servants of some nice feelings then we are actually slaves to the demands of the body and mind. We're not really free to be the best we can be."

Listening askance as young teenagers do, Priya seemed more convinced.

"Pot is not in our own best interest," I said. "In the end smoking it won't make us happy or healthy. And no one should think that smoking

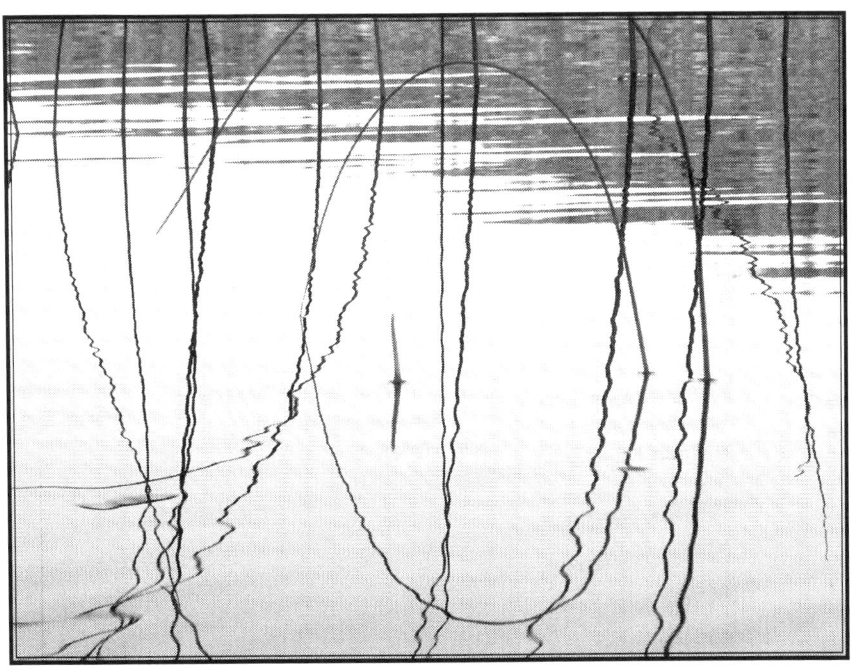

pot won't affect them in the long term. Pot often leads to stronger, more addictive drugs. I'd like to remind our pot-smoking neighbor of all these things too."

Priya seemed to understand. We hoped our pot-smoking neighbor would give up his pot, but somehow or other people problems, like animal and bug problems, seem to sort themselves out where nature predominates.

Bhagavad-gita says, "God does not assume anyone's sinful or pious activities" (5.15). And no one else is responsible for what we do either. The circumstances in which we find ourselves are due to us. The knower of Bhagavad-gita does not blame or accuse or complain about anyone or anything for the situation he or she is in. I am personally responsible for my own situation. There are no accidents in God's creation.

I'm free to the degree that I correctly discern the best course of action and can act in accord with who I am. Yet even in this freedom I am helpless – due to my smallness – but helpless before God instead of poor choices. In being responsible for myself and yet dependent on God, I can come closer to Him and He to me.

Week after week as the ice on our windshield thickened, my family and I were stoking our wood stove and passing convivial evenings warming our hearts discussing Bhagavad-gita in the company of Sharanagati-ites. The cold, instead of being prohibitive, was providing a cozy ambience in which we could shrink the distances between us. Those distances, it seemed, were waiting patiently for us to shrink them.

*Don't blame your fate on others; your behavior determines your own fate.*

— The Tao

*"Discrimination is the best part of valor." Simply we have to learn how to discriminate whether we are working on the material platform or on the*

*spiritual platform. That's all. Just like Arjuna. Arjuna was being advised to work on the spiritual platform. The whole instruction of Bhagavad-gita is based on this principle, that Arjuna was perplexed with material thoughts. And Lord Krishna wanted to place him in the spiritual platform. So, from Arjuna's activity, you can understand that what is the spiritual platform and what is the material platform.*

— Bhaktivedanta Swami Prabhupada

**Knowing oneself to be transcendental to the material senses, mind and intelligence, one should steady the mind by deliberate spiritual intelligence and thus – by spiritual strength – conquer the insatiable enemy known as lust. 3.43**

## Illusion

On one of my long walks through Sharanagati I came near a herd of about fifty grazing cows, calves and bulls. As I watched, an enormous, mean-looking gray-and-black bull snorted, dug the earth with his front hoof and began chasing a frightened brown-and-white heifer, which darted in and out of the herd and lost herself. The bull paused, turned and then lumbered after another larger heifer, which also ran away. Despite his size, this time the bull moved fast. At the same time another bull rushed to the right side of the pursued heifer, lowered his head and rammed into her. (Fortunately this bull didn't have horns.) The heifer finally stood still in acquiescence. The gray-black beast mounted and injected himself into her, and a minute later all three animals were calmly grazing with the rest of the herd.

What happened between those bulls and heifers is what happens in numberless interactions between males and females of all species

throughout the world. We humans, however, make the raw reproductive urge that serves to regenerate each species endlessly complex. Instinct obliges most animals to provide for their young, but we often fail to be responsible for the result of our sexual exploits – not only the child who may be conceived, but also the emotional bond between us and our partner and the practical needs that result from our union.

Lust, a tyrant of limitless demands, plunders the fort of the body to degrade the *jivatma*:

> While contemplating the objects of the senses, a person develops attachment for them, and from such attachment lust develops,

> and from lust anger arises. From anger, complete delusion arises, and from delusion bewilderment of memory.
>
> — Bhagavad-gita 2.62–63

When Arjuna asks Krishna, "By what is one impelled to immoral acts, even unwillingly, as if engaged by force?" Krishna answers,

> It is lust only, Arjuna … the all-devouring sinful enemy of this world.
>
> — Bhagavad-gita 3.37

Bhaktivedanta Swami Prabhupada comments: "Lust is the greatest enemy of the living entity, and it is lust only which induces the pure living entity to remain entangled in the material world."

In the twenty-first century we no longer struggle against rigid moral codes but against our own depravity and the cravings that so overwhelm us that we can justify or overlook almost anything, including blatant and destructive acts.

Lust shackles the *jivatma* in selfish desires and invokes enmity between people.

Love frees the *jivatma* of lust and evokes harmony between people.

> The desire to gratify one's own senses is lust, but the desire to please God's senses is love. The object of lust is only the enjoyment of one's own senses. But love caters to the enjoyment of God, and thus it is very powerful.... Therefore lust and love are quite different. Lust is like dense darkness, but love is like the bright sun.
>
> — Chaitanya Charitamrita 1.4.165–166, 171

As the earth rotates on its axis and the Sharanagati seasons revolve, gradually I – a *jivatma* – accept that material things, whatever their shape or qualities, are ultimately unworthy of my deepest feelings of love. Love, like the *jivatma,* is eternal and is meant for the eternal. Love, the bonding force of selfless caring, has nothing to do with matter. It is the emotion between spirit and spirit. It is about what I, a *jivatma,* can do for you, a *jivatma.* So my love for my husband and daughter is not really for their minds or intelligence, which go through many changes, or for their bodies, which go through many phases. In the midst of these changes and phases, the intimate, warm radiance of my love finds no repose until it finally comes to *jivatma,* the eternal living force within the body of my husband and daughter. As it's the *jivatma* that loves, so it's also the *jivatma* that is lovable.

When the body, mind and intelligence of my husband and daughter change, as they inevitably will, I may find those changes agreeable or disagreeable. Yet I want to love others, especially my husband and daughter, steadily. So I practice loving them for their benefit and pleasure instead of mine. Then even if my "approval rating" of them drops, my love isn't affected. That's not to say that I must agree with what they do; it means I learn to see past their behavior.

True love is not exploitative. It means that I think of my beloved's gratification and my beloved thinks of my gratification. True love is without motive: I may enjoy or not but I love. In my life true love is still a theory, but a theory I'm drawn to explore and experience.

Bhagavad-gita challenges me to transform lust into love. But lust is so strong that unless I'm determined, even God Himself cannot protect me from it. Yet, success is possible, as Bhaktivedanta Swami says:

> By austerity, you have to change that lust into love. If you love one girl, if you love one boy, that is very nice. That is natural. That is not unnatural. But don't change that love. Be combined permanently. Be combined. Not that "After a few months I give up this girl," "I give up this boy," "I capture another." No. That is austerity.

Marriage is more than just an arrangement to please me and my spouse; it is a way to serve God. In the early, cold morning of November 29, 1971, in the little Indian village of Vrindavan, 90 miles south of Delhi, Bhaktivedanta Swami presided over my marriage with John. In the decades since then our relationship has known ripples, joggles, bumps and explosions, but beyond the sweet and tough times it has also helped us expand from me-centered to thee-centered to Thee-centered and to all-of-you-out-there-centered living.

As John and I have slowly become flexible and patient with each other's fluctuations and idiosyncrasies, so have we become flexible and patient with those around us. We witness a child's tantrums and then her tenderness; we empathize with a teenager's anger and with her contrition months later. We see marriages and separations, one person's reflective communion and another's suspicion, one's genuine affection and another's ceaseless criticism. We note changing loyalties and the waxing and waning of good and bad habits.

By consistently desiring the best for each person, including ourselves, these diverse emotions become like fall storms against a majestic mountain. As that mountain weathers and beautifies the wind and water, so transcendent knowledge purifies the turbulence of lust and reveals gentle, selfless love. Together, we Sharanagati-ites want to look past the vacillating mind and the ever-changing body to the glorious love of the *jivatma* within.

> Different people are of different mentalities. Therefore it is not my business either to praise them or to blaspheme them. I only desire their welfare, hoping that they will agree to become one in purpose with God.
>
> — Srimad-Bhagavatam 7.13.42

*Every act is either a call for love or an expression of love.*

— Bhakti Tirtha Swami

**Just try to learn the truth by approaching a spiritual master. Submissively inquire from and render service unto that person. The self-realized souls can impart knowledge to you because they have seen the truth. 4.34**

## Inspiration

One lazy summer afternoon John, never one to miss a deal, came home with a one-person, orange-and-white, seven-foot-long fiberglass kayak in the back of our minivan.

"I couldn't pass it up," he said.

At first I looked askance at this new possession, but after John and Priya tried it and said it was a ton of fun, I also took it out on Lake Sharanagati. In a few minutes I learned the rhythm of paddling and then was off, tooling from end to end of our mile-long lake, exploring marshes that before I had only seen from a distance and obliging families of mallards to take flight. As waves lapped beside me and sunlight sparkled and danced on the dark green water I thought of an ancient yet applicable analogy:

> This human body can be compared to a perfectly constructed boat having the guru as the captain and God's instructions as favorable winds impelling it on its course.
>
> — Srimad-Bhagavatam 11.20.17

The boat of the body needs a captain – the guru – and a companionable breeze – Bhagavad-gita. When I was twenty years old and John twenty-seven, we were in Mumbai when we heard from Bhaktivedanta Swami Prabhupada and our lives were revolutionized. John's mother was a Christian Scientist and his father an agnostic, but both my parents were atheists and, except to appreciate the architecture or stained glass, I'd never gone into a church, temple or mosque. Neither had I read any scripture. All my life I'd considered religious people addled, and after debates with my best friend I eventually got her to question her formerly impassioned Catholicism. Bhaktivedanta Swami, however, avoided all arguments with me and instead suggested that John and I go to Vrindavan, India's holiest town, where the residents' guileless trust in God won John over and even permeated my crusty heart. I began to think, "Maybe there is something to this God stuff," and the world began to make more sense than it had before. Life's mysteries and majesties pushed, poked and pried me open, just a sliver, to the inconceivable lovable Person Bhaktivedanta Swami Prabhupada spoke and wrote about.

> By the grace of God one who is fortunate gets an opportunity to associate with a bona fide guru. By the mercy of both God and guru, such a person receives the seed of spiritual life.
>
> — Chaitanya Charitamrita 2.19.151

Spiritual life begins with hearing transcendent knowledge from a person who has accepted a spiritual teacher and whose life is an expression of that person's teachings – teachings based on scriptural tenets. With kindness the guru, who is not a self-made authority but part of a lineage of gurus, evokes spiritual enthusiasm in his or her students.

> The bona fide guru is one who has realized the conclusions of the scriptures by deliberation and is able to convince others of these conclusions. Such great personalities have taken shelter of God, leaving aside all worldly considerations.
>
> — Srimad-Bhagavatam 11.3.21

Because time and again I'd seen cheaters disguised as gurus, I had a cynical view of the guru principle and zero interest in finding a guru. But, after I'd somehow heard from a genuine guru, I could see how much I needed him: the guru's words offered me direction and guided me past turbulent distractions; the guru's example inspired me to improve. The guru, a friend like no other, was more a well-wisher of mine than I was of myself.

A qualified guru is rare, and finding such a person is only half the challenge. The other half is becoming a qualified seeker. In the '70s I had some healthy skepticism about my then current attainments and life itinerary. Although I'd published a commercially successful book at age twenty and had had a solo exhibit of photographs in New York City a couple of months later, as I flew to India to join John I had a sense of vacancy. Life had given me everything I wanted, yet something vital was missing. My wants, I thought, must be awry. But how? What should I want? I was adrift. Bhaktivedanta Swami, with ease and sometimes with humor, offered me the awareness that I was more than my everyday external self; he claimed that I was (and that everyone is) one in quality with God, who is beyond all that's mundane. Bhaktivedanta Swami's gift was not a single event but a dynamic continuum of inner clarity. An example of his own guru's values and behavior, Bhaktivedanta Swami stirred in me a desire for the happiness and harmony he knew. The process, he said, begins simply by my hearing about God. And it continues simply by remembering what I've heard. Even when I'm paddling around a lake in a kayak.

*Religion thrives when leaders offer inspiring possibilities and rich interpretations of experience; when they truly help us deal responsibly and hopefully with our mortality, our attempts at love, and our work; and when we can admire them and wish to be like them rather than follow their stipulations out of fear or contest them in rebellion. We want real spiritual guidance. Such a person can help us to become what we potentially are – not what he or she wants us to be.*

— Thomas Moore

*No men are more unfortunate or nearer perdition than those who have no teachers on the way of God. For what does it mean that where no guidance is, the people fall like leaves? A leaf is at first green, flourishing, beautiful, then it gradually withers, falls, and is finally trampled underfoot. So it is with the man who has no guide.*

— St. Dorotheus (7th-century Eastern Orthodox Christian)

*Our only hope is to make our consciousness one with the words of the guru. Do not consider anything else in your mind.*

— Narottam das Thakur

**In this world, there is nothing so sublime and pure as transcendental knowledge. Such knowledge is the mature fruit of all mysticism. 4.38**

## Wisdom

If I remember who I am – *jivatma* – I'll have the fortitude to cast aside mundane concepts.

Spiritual enlightenment means to first try to understand the *jivatma*, the small particle of the Lord. If you test a small particle of gold, then you can understand the composition of

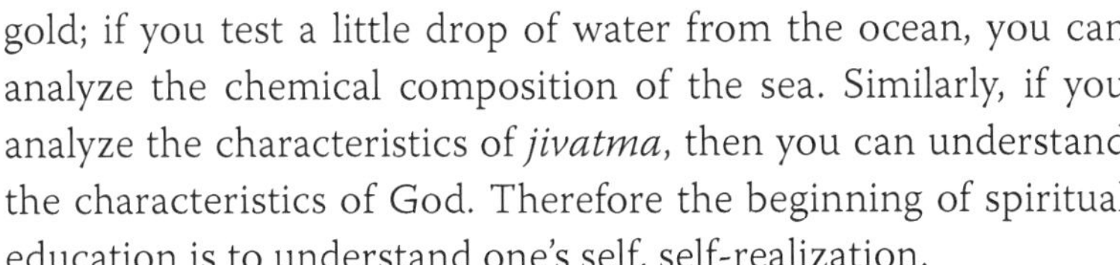
gold; if you test a little drop of water from the ocean, you can analyze the chemical composition of the sea. Similarly, if you analyze the characteristics of *jivatma*, then you can understand the characteristics of God. Therefore the beginning of spiritual education is to understand one's self, self-realization.

— Bhaktivedanta Swami Prabhupada

Wisdom – realized knowledge of *jivatma* and the world it lives in – is not just a theoretical understanding but is an unveiling of what is actually important. As a red-winged blackbird naturally sings its cheerful song, so with wisdom comes natural inner cheer. As the hearty sound from a lone bird fills our home, so when we know just one thing – our spiritual identity – in truth, we are inundated by that perception.

Wisdom, the heart's ecstasy in the charm of the simple truth, is not a product of cleverness or of amassing information or of intellectual prowess. It's a gift that I can sometimes sense just by the gratitude I feel, both for the life I'm leading and for the insights that give my life meaning and hope. Sometimes wisdom makes itself known through the surprising sense that there's no one anywhere with whom I wish to trade places. And sometimes wisdom's fullness lets controversies, setbacks and mishaps leave me unfazed. Such glimpses of wisdom's riches leave me hankering for more.

*I have suspected, more often than not, that I know more than [my grandmother] did, that I know more than my grandfather and my great-grandmother did, but I also know that I'm no wiser than they were.*

— Toni Morrison

*The wise man is he who has thoroughly understood that he is spirit soul and not simply a body.*

— Bhaktivedanta Swami Prabhupada

2

# Harmony with the Earth and Her Creatures

*Having probed our eternal spiritual essence –* jivatma *– we seek harmony with the creatures of the earth by honoring that spiritual essence in all beings. We view the creation as one would view a rare and priceless gemstone – pondering its innumerable facets, marveling at its existence and treasuring it and the great mystery of its unseen Creator.*

**A complete analytical study of the material world causes one to act in concert with its Creator. 5.4**

## Our World

Far removed from throngs of city-dwellers who move against backdrops of concrete, glass and steel, my lonely walks on Sharanagati's winding cow paths evoke a central truth: my spiritual well-being rests on the quality of my relationship with the Creator and His creation.

Here in Sharanagati the innumerable beings in innumerable species that surround me unerringly obey nature's laws. I am part of that nature yet unique, in that unlike the beings in all other species, as a human I can become self-aware. Slowly, by analyzing the varied aspects of this good, uncluttered place, I want to sense the living force – the *jivatma* – that shines beyond superficialities.

My days here start with pre-dawn mantra meditation and Bhagavad-gita study. Later I help my daughter get off to school and my husband to his nearby film editing studio, and then I write, garden, do household chores and try to apply the Gita's wisdom by awakening to the absolutely sublime nature of absolutely ordinary things. The Creator is not remote and esoteric, but is available daily, hourly and second-by-second; awareness of Him, evoked in inner stillness, can be as private and essential as breathing.

> I am the taste of water, the light of the sun and the moon, the syllable om in the Vedic mantras; I am the sound in ether and ability in man. I am the original fragrance of the earth, and I am the heat in fire. I am the life of all that lives, and I am the penance of all ascetics. I am the original seed of all existences, the intelligence of the intelligent, and the prowess of all powerful people.
>
> — Bhagavad-gita 7.8–10, Krishna speaking

When I pause from gardening to take in the moment, the conversation of the magpies and the breeze wafting through the fir needles, the valley that extends before me and the life-giving richness and sweetness of the compost in my hands, all resound around and through me. To be present is to participate in a celebration.

Wherever we are, we can respond to the spirit's yearning for fulfillment by accepting a mood of stewardship. Even in a city we can remain aware that all raw materials – sand, water, air, metal, fire – come from God and adjust our environment to help this remembrance. To beautify our surroundings, to avoid wasting resources and simply to care is to let the Gita's teachings bring harmony to our daily life. Something as unsophisticated as a potted fern in our office or herbs and flowers on

our windowsill can remind us of the reality of harmony. We begin to see our place and the beings in it as part of God's creation, a creation in which everything matters. We tolerate inevitable discomforts – heat, cold, congestion, isolation, overwhelming expenses, noise, pollution, monotony – and we live on this earth not to rule but to serve and to allow our identity to be unveiled. We are, after all, beings of modest intelligence that can never fully know or control the world we live in, but who can summon a sense of awe for God's artistry. As our admiration for the Creator grows, so does our respect for His creation.

In this mood of stewardship I live as a softer person, accepting trials and favors that come with conditions I cannot foresee or direct, from a place I cannot ascertain, and that aren't subject to my tyrannical orders. For me to fulfill my deepest needs takes a favor of grace, for whatever I can get only by my own efforts is, in the end, not what I really seek.

To meet my true needs, for a meaningful life and for lasting love, I'm called on to relax the mental and intellectual walls that confine me to the material "I" that is all I presently know of as myself. That is, I'm to open myself to a miracle.

> Because of his development of transcendental attachment for God, a surrendered soul feels the presence of his beloved everywhere, and all his senses are engaged in the loving service of the Lord.
>
> — Bhaktivedanta Swami Prabhupada

With grace and warmth, the Bhagavad-gita connects me to completeness, to the Creator of that completeness and to my own resplendent spiritual identity; with profound cogency the Gita inspires me to cooperate with the Creator's creation. And I can try to do that even as I plant cherry tomato seedlings in the small, fertile garden in front of our home.

*The world is designed to present the mind with a fundamental moral choice as well as a dilemma whose only solution lies in an acknowledgment of, and encounter with, God.*

— Patrick Glynn

*When we wear blue spectacles everything appears blue; by seeing everything in relation to guru and Krishna, we come to see everything through divine vision. Everything will rightly appear worshipable. This universe is full of objects for the service of the master of this universe. Therefore, all objects are worshipable ... I am meant to serve and worship this material world, which is meant for the universal Father's enjoyment.*

— Bhaktisiddhanta Sarasvati Thakur

*What artists call beautiful nature is but God's smile, and what they call the sweet songs of the birds are but specimens of the whispering voice of God ...*

— Srimad-Bhagavatam 1.11.26

**Those who work in devotion, who are pure souls, and who control their mind and senses are dear to everyone, and everyone is dear to them. 5.7**

## Nearness to Others

After an infestation of grasshoppers plagued us for two summers, we Sharanagati-ites fought back. Bluebirds feast on grasshoppers, and to encourage these birds to reside among us we organized a community bluebird-house-building day. After that, each family had ten bluebird houses to hang around their home, and sometime later I was pleased to see a bluebird couple frequenting a house I'd hung on a fence post just thirty feet from our living room. Then, unexpectedly, one sunny July afternoon I saw that birdhouse had somehow fallen off its nail and was lying face down on the ground. I picked it up and opened its door to find five distressed baby bluebirds huddled on top of each other inside. Fortunately there was another, unused bluebird house two fence posts north, so one by one I used a stick to nudge each baby onto a plastic lid (I didn't want to touch them, for I'd heard that birds reject chicks who have a human scent) and then deposited it into the other birdhouse. This worked for four of the chicks, but the fifth one was more developed and half flew, half jumped south. When I'd finished moving its four siblings, I went looking for this fifth bird, which by that time had gone many yards. Suddenly out of the clear sky, the mother bluebird swooped down on me with beady black eyes, a needle-sharp small black beak and a vengeance. I ducked low. She turned and swooped down again; I

ducked low again. After the third or fourth attack I gave up my search for her lost chick and ran into the house, slamming the door behind me. Now the mother bluebird flew back and forth where her house had been, unable to find her chicks. I went out again and stood by the new birdhouse, thinking that if she attacked me she'd find the new house. It didn't work. So I picked up the old, fallen house and put it directly under the new one. She still flew back and forth over the old location. I gave up, went inside and some three hours later looked out to see the mother bluebird going into and out of the new birdhouse. Success! But those four baby birds had been without food for hours; at least the weakest one, I was sure, would die. Some weeks later I saw three chicks perched in the birdhouse opening and, with binoculars, watched them simultaneously open their three mouths as wide as their entire heads when their loyal mother flew by. Without landing she stuffed food into one open mouth and continued flying in search of more food. It was a fast-food flyby. I was convinced that the fourth bird was dead inside the house, but a couple of weeks after that, when there was no more bird activity, I opened the house and found it empty. I'd somehow saved the lives of four bluebirds, and who knew how many hundreds of descendants those birds would have in generations to come. It was my teeny contribution to a colossal ecological system.

The Gita confirms a reality I'd already deeply felt: that I am not estranged from other living beings but, in my individual, core identity, have a bond with them as they do with me and with each other. I have a spiritual alliance with each and every living being.

Under the direction of a single and personal Creator there's a divine plan for each *jivatma*, and part of my role in this plan is to avoid causing anxiety to any living thing, regardless of how insignificant that living thing may seem. We respond to the will of the Creator by honoring others' rights, thus sharing His care for them.

> Because one who works in Krishna consciousness is servant to all, he is very dear to everyone. And because everyone is satisfied by his work, he is pure in consciousness. Because he is pure in consciousness, his mind is completely controlled. And because his mind is controlled, his senses are also controlled.
>
> — Bhaktivedanta Swami Prabhupada

Nearness to others pries me away from self-infatuation and lets me see them on their terms. As I respect myself I also respect another. Just trying to relate on this level reveals that, in one sense, no position in this material world is more or less important than any other position. And it reveals that promoting nature's balances is a viable, life-friendly (except to the grasshoppers) alternative to using harmful chemicals.

The happiness of everyone being dear to me rests in my will. And that happiness releases the magic of harmony: daily dealings become as heartening as a child's spontaneous laughter.

*With so much more to learn, looking around, we should be more embarrassed than we are. We are different [from other species], to be sure, but not so much because of our brains as because of our discomfiture, mostly with each other. All the other parts of the earth's life seem to get along, to fit in with each other, to accommodate, even to concede when the stakes are high.*

— Lewis Thomas

*Harmony is inevitable when we consider that everything is to be enjoyed by Krishna.*

— Chaitanya Bhagavat 2.15.7

**The humble sages, by virtue of true knowledge, see with equal vision a learned and gentle scholar, a cow, an elephant, a dog and a dog-eater. 5.18**

## Equal Vision

> There is a sweet transcendental interrelation between all living entities irrespective of not only caste, creed and color between man and man, but also between man and beast, man and birds, man and reptiles, man and plants, as well as between man and God, and between God and others. The Bhagavad-gita can scientifically raise this standard of sweet relations between one thing and another ... neither God nor the living being nor nature is in any way antagonistic toward one another, but all of them exist in harmony as a complete whole unit.... There is no other practical solution for universal brotherhood or universal religion without understanding the simple truth of the fatherhood of God, motherhood of Nature, and childhood of all living entities. The unity of all life is affirmed.
>
> — Bhaktivedanta Swami Prabhupada

Before we moved to Sharanagati, my family and I used to visit my in-laws in Corona del Mar, a posh coastal town south of Los Angeles. One morning while walking past the most elite of the beachfront houses, I noticed a magnificent, rambling dark-wooden house with a large lawn and three Rolls Royces in the driveway. As I was looking, a woman walked up to the front gate and called in a friendly way. A moment later the homeowner, teacup in hand, opened her front door, smiled, strolled across the spacious porch, and went down the steps and along a lily-lined path to chat with her friend.

The homeowner was about my height and age, had my coloring and build and was casually dressed, as I was. Yet, I marveled, her monthly income might very well equal my yearly income. At that moment I realized how, although houses may differ vastly, as do the many life species – huge, tiny, ugly, colorful, plain, strong, complex, simple, aristocratic, primitive – within each house is a person who is equal to the person in any other house, just as that homeowner and I were equal in so many ways. Similarly, the *jivatma* in one body is equal in quality and quantity to the *jivatma* in any other body, whatever the species. Where there is life a *jivatma* is present, and every *jivatma* is created equally and equally lives with God.

> God is conscious, as is the living being, but the living being is conscious of his particular body, whereas God is conscious of all bodies. Because He lives in the heart of every living being, He is conscious of the psychic movements of the particular *jivatmas.*
>
> — Bhaktivedanta Swami Prabhupada

As the Supersoul – Paramatma – God is the constant companion of the *jivatma*. Supersoul is equally friendly with every *jivatma* and remains with the *jivatma* regardless of its circumstances. Every living entity in all forms of life is a *jivatma* accompanied by Supersoul – God Himself. As grown-up brothers and sisters take pleasure in each other's company, so each *jivatma* is ever worthy of filial affection. This natural affection evolves and gives pleasure to the Father, Supersoul, as our narcissism dissolves. Before I became interested in spiritual life, I wouldn't have crossed paths with most of the Sharanagati neighbors I have today. We would have moved in different circles. Yet now I can see how, in their own right, each one of them is attractive and has much to offer.

The soul and the Supersoul in the body, *jivatma* and Paramatma, are of the same spiritual quality although they are not equal in quantity:

> The similar characteristics of the soul and Supersoul are that they are both conscious, eternal and blissful. But the difference is that the individual soul is conscious within the limited jurisdiction of the body whereas the Supersoul is conscious of all bodies. The Supersoul is present in all bodies without distinction.
>
> — Bhaktivedanta Swami Prabhupada

In its deepest essence, every living thing is spiritual. As I quietly observe the host of diverse beings around me, I find myself marveling at, and learning from, all of them.

*We have tried on a large scale the experiment of preferring ourselves to the exclusion of all other creatures, with results that are manifestly disastrous.... The problem obviously is that we are not well practiced in kindness toward our fellow humans. In the course of our unprecedented inhumanity toward other creatures and the world, we have become unprecedentedly inhumane toward humans.*

— Wendell Berry

*The more uncertain I have felt about myself, the more there has grown up in me a feeling of kinship with all things.*

— C. G. Jung

*Bugs that eat our crops aren't doing it to be 'bad,' of course; they're just trying to survive, like everybody else! Their choice of food is what got them their bad name. Other bugs, the kind that eat the 'bad' ones, are thought of as 'good.' Get it? This kind of bad-good thinking doesn't reflect the whole truth, of course – that bugs and insects are a part of nature and have the right to be here.*

— Avery Hart and Paul Mantell ***(Kid's Garden!)***

**A person in full consciousness of Me, knowing Me to be the Supreme Lord and the ultimate enjoyer of everything, as well as the friend of all living entities, attains peace from the pangs of all misgivings. 5.29**

## Peace

Sometimes people look at photos of Sharanagati and say, "Oh, it looks so peaceful. No wonder you live there!" Others see the same photos and say, "How can you live there? What do you do there?" When this second type visit, their minds are brimming with the urgent things they must do elsewhere, and the unrest in their heart, which remains camouflaged by their travels and the cacophony of urban living, surges up like blustery fall winds. Settling into Sharanagati's stillness was not easy for me either. When we first moved here I was nervous. What would I do alone in the house all day during the long winter's icy quiet? Would my mind drive me nuts? But it turned out that I learned to laugh at my mind's lurching antics; my mind was a cross between a defiant child, a grouch, a critic and a bum. No wonder peace – normality – seemed impossibly impractical.

The peace of Sharanagati, like all genuine peace, is not the anesthesia of complacency. Neither is it the proud swell of self-indulgence or the dullness of blind acceptance or a shirking of responsibility or an escape from conflict. Rather, the peace we find here can be transported anywhere, as it rests on the *jivatma's* indigenous quality: confidence in God.

One who has attained this peace will still know the ongoing self-scrutiny and uncertainty, the perceptive inquiry and sincere endeavor that are integral to the spiritual quest. A desire for fame and wealth can so distort this quest that the resulting dissatisfaction puts us at war with ourselves and others. False expectations dismantle peace; acceptance of our lot in life restores it.

The peace offered in Bhagavad-gita is not the end of commotion but the end of selfish living, the end of separation and disunity. That peace is evoked in the *jivatma* who is no longer awash in conflicting ideologies. That peace is for one who is neither a slave of passion and hedonism nor a robot of conventions submerged in trivia. That peace is for those who have forgotten themselves in the humility of offering themselves to the service of God and who accept His plan. In the past few years an infestation of pine beetles, a product of global warming, has littered Sharanagati with dead pines. We mill some of the trees for lumber, cut some for firewood and have reconciled ourselves with our valley's pervasive dead-tree look. We residents may not be responsible for this ecological mess, but we've found that dealing with it starts a current of acceptance.

As I continue to accept who I am – an indestructible, immortal *jivatma* – that current of acceptance becomes a current of happiness and harmony. Understanding that I have a relationship with God and His creatures, aspiring for nothing extraneous, with a joyous heart I firmly relinquish my former mad, empty life and become rooted in my new one.

God is the recipient of all offerings, the master of all creation, and everyone's friend and well-wisher. Peace is the fruit of my acceptance of and submission to His will. Peace is His gift to me from the trust I place in Him. This doesn't mean that my life is free of conflict (or of pine beetles), but that peace gifts me much-needed patience. And Sharanagati issues, like most issues, require patience. Whether we're discussing our children's schooling, or the use and care of our animals and land and water, or interfacing with residents of other valleys, or our roads and budget and fund-raising programs, as we mediate our differences we remain under one overarching goal: to somehow make our decisions worthy of our concealed identity – *jivatma*.

Life can be a spiritual journey undertaken with hope, self-discipline and a God-conscious guide. One who so journeys achieves peace, although peace is not the goal of the journey but an afterthought – like the complimentary orchid the airline steward gives you when you land in Hawaii.

*Remember that you are an actor in a play; your business is to act your part well. To choose your part is another's business.*

— Epictetus

*Thou wilt keep him in perfect peace, whose mind is stayed on Thee.*

— Isaiah 26:3

**For him who has conquered the mind, the mind is the best of friends; but for one who has failed to do so, his mind will remain the greatest enemy. 6.6**

## No Mind Trips

In Sharanagati's dense forests all I hear is the soft, steady fall of my footsteps on the thick duff. The air is clear and invigorating, tinged with scents from seas of firs. Sunlight, glowing and shimmering between boughs, occasionally bursts through small openings in the canopy. Part of the forest's beauty is its tangled wildness: conifers with low-lying and interlocking limbs (that make ladders for fire to climb), crowded crops of saplings that block the way, dead trees scattered on the ground among the living ones like fallen monarchs of a previous era.

The fires that periodically ravage a forest are part of the ecosystem, and each year as new fuel falls, the forest cries a little louder to be cleared by devastation. Only we Sharanagati-ites see all that drying fuel and anxiously hope that the forest's cries go unanswered. Toward the end of each arid summer our prayers become especially fervent.

Yet, at all times and in all places, we live with a graver threat:

> The soul's designation, the mind, is the cause of all tribulations in the material world.
>
> — Srimad-Bhagavatam 5.11.16

The mind, like the forest, is God's energy:

> Earth, water, fire, air, ether, mind, intelligence and false ego – all together these eight constitute My separated material energies.
>
> — Bhagavad-gita 7.4, Krishna speaking

We think, feel and will with the mind, we accept or reject what our senses perceive with the mind and, like an unkempt forest, the mind may endanger us. Destructive emotions, fanaticism, warped desires, attachment to profit and acclaim create the dangerous clutter that stifles an interior life, that kills balance and sanity.

> This uncontrolled mind is the greatest enemy of the living entity. If one gives it a chance, it will grow more and more powerful and will become victorious.
>
> — Srimad-Bhagavatam 5.11.17

To control the mind, however, is not easy:

> The mind is restless, turbulent, obstinate and very strong, O Krishna, and to subdue it, I think, is more difficult than controlling the wind.
>
> — Bhagavad-gita 6.34, Arjuna speaking

Before the forest fire in the summer of '03, we'd been lax to the threat that lurks in a forest; the following fall we became proactive. With saw and rake in hand we limbed, thinned, chopped back brush, gathered fallen logs, branches and pinecones and burned them all in dozens of massive piles in a wide ring around our home. When the smoke cleared, for the first time we could see the gentle contours of the land and watch the dappled sunlight spill onto the grassy, spacious areas between the trees. Neighbors said our property looked like a park – but to keep it that way I have to regularly pile and burn. To keep a park wildness-free takes ongoing effort.

The mind also needs ongoing supervision. We're not obliged to succumb to its narrow and exploitive aspect that's sometimes cheerful and sometimes miserable, that's ingrown and subject to depression, that can cast us down into a bleaker place than we can imagine. Presided over, that same mind can also uplift us beyond our imaginings.

> For one who has conquered the mind, the Supersoul is already reached, for that person has attained tranquility. To such a person happiness and distress, heat and cold, honor and dishonor are all the same.
>
> — Bhagavad-gita 6.7

The mind, however, isn't controlled by technology, religious rituals, conformity, mundane learning, physical strength, wealth, fame, popularity or prestige.

> Krishna said: O Arjuna, it is undoubtedly very difficult to curb the restless mind, but it is possible by suitable practice and by detachment.
>
> — Bhagavad-gita 6.35

Teeming with desires and demands, jumping at imagined hints, puzzling over random thoughts, the mind puts forward concerns and ditties, longings, self-reproaches and mixed-up feelings every waking hour and, ever so rarely, has some original and generous notion. Practice and detachment enable us to sort through this wild forest, pile up unhelpful thoughts and burn them in the fire of neglect. When heaps of mental clutter are reduced to ashes, the fires of mental anguish die for want of fuel. We are happy.

> The mind is always telling us to do this or that; therefore we should be very expert in disobeying the mind's orders. Gradually the mind should be trained to obey the orders of the soul. It is not that one should obey the orders of the mind.
>
> — Bhaktivedanta Swami Prabhupada

Knowledge is the basis of happiness and harmony with the earth and her creatures. With knowledge, we – *jivatma* – predominate over the incredibly powerful mind and soon discover that open and sunlit space where, with a light heart, we can freely dedicate ourselves to a higher cause.

*From the accumulated sadness into which I fell, I had at length no hope of ever issuing again. I roamed from place to place, carrying my burden with me everywhere. I felt its whole weight now, and I drooped beneath it, and I said in my heart that it could never be lightened. When this despondency was at its worst, I believed that I should die ... It is not in my power to retrace, one by one, all the weary phases of distress of mind through which I passed.*

— Charles Dickens *(David Copperfield)*

*This wicked mind, which is never to be trusted, should be broomsticked every morning with such warnings as, 'Be not anxious to find fault with others, or to declare thyself a true sincere, bona fide devotee, which certainly thou art not!' A man who is habituated to criticize others' conduct will never prosper. Let others do whatever they like, I have no concern for them. I should rather find fault with my own damned mind.*

— Bhaktisiddhanta Sarasvati Thakur

*After capturing animals, a cunning hunter does not put faith in them, for they might run away. Similarly, those who are advanced in spiritual life do not put faith in the mind. Indeed, they always remain vigilant and watch the mind's action. All the learned scholars have given their opinion. The mind is by nature very restless, and one should not make friends with it. If we place full confidence in the mind, it may cheat us at any moment.*

— Srimad-Bhagavatam 5.6.2–3

*Everything, spiritual and material, depends on one's mental condition.*

— Srimad-Bhagavatam 10.10.4

**He who is temperate in his habits of eating, sleeping, recreation and work can mitigate all material pains by practicing the yoga system. 6.17**

## Balance

Although outwardly uneventful, my Sharanagati days are peculiarly happy. Each spring, as warmth slowly returns, the life potency of the fallow land revitalizes me and gives me joy. Summer's long days, filled with relatives, friends and guests, with weddings, retreats, seminars, festivals, boating, hiking, swimming and the garden's bounty, are busy times I relish looking back on. When fall arrives my heart aches – but with a certain sweetness – as I rediscover the contented solitude that fills the cool emptiness. And as winter closes in, the land, also alone, lies untouched, and its quiet forbearance, its range of beauty, its solemn serenity pervades me. In Sharanagati it's easier to remember nature's diverse and graceful balance. My awareness of this divine balance, whose truth doesn't need outside validation, grounds me and thickens my connection to the sacred.

Why was my awareness feeble before? Rather than the rhythms of planting, tending, harvesting and hibernating, for me Los Angeles life

meant the harshness of working at something I had little interest in. It meant a layer of concrete separating me from mother earth's possibilities of life, the hypnotic effect of being ever steeped in a nonstop drone of traffic with its rush-hour crescendos. Now I realize that the mere noise of city life from the ardent, endless endeavor of millions of drivers, its mechanized smell, the glare from its lights that obliterates the night stars, the vast emotional distances that separate its dwellers, block deeper and more pleasing perceptions.

Balance pervades the universe and all it contains. In Sharanagati I see it in the movements of the planets in the night sky; I feel it in my war with weeds; I observe it in the relationships between the bears and the ants; I sense it in the care bluebird parents show their young; I even notice it in our pine beetle and grasshopper sagas, as well as in my exchanges with neighbors.

By becoming a sincere, simple serving component in God's all-serving climate I personally experience this balance – His balance.

This service attitude is the diametric opposite of exploitation; this service attitude is a unique privilege. Knowing that my body is a temple in which God – Paramatma – resides with me – *jivatma* – I have the opportunity to turn to Him and ask, "What can I do for You?" And with this attitude, dissatisfaction, which is the wellspring of imbalance, evaporates.

Part of what I can do for God is to serve my physical body. Since God resides within it, it's a temple. To neglect the body and tend only to the spirit is foolishness, and to neglect the spirit and tend only to the body is ignorance. So without overendeavor or overindulgence I meet the needs of my body, my mind and me – a *jivatma* – and in so doing am progressively released from the upheavals of imbalance. With this healthy foundation I can weather any extraordinary turmoil that goes on around or inside me.

When my body and mind cooperate with me, my path is clear; without that cooperation I'm confused and make poor choices. I am, after all, an ordinary person with innumerable desires, and this world is a warehouse of materials to fulfill those desires. These materials are not intrinsically good or bad; rather, it's my disposition toward them and how I use them that determines the effect they have on me. With discretion I choose between my desires, accepting what is favorable and rejecting what is unfavorable for my internal and external life.

Daily tasks and creative acts – done with attention and a mood of service to God – satisfy Him and also deeply satisfy me.

> Work done as a sacrifice for God has to be performed; otherwise work causes bondage in this material world. Therefore, perform your prescribed duties for His satisfaction, and in that way you will always remain free from bondage.
>
> — Bhagavad-gita 3.9

To be sublimely motivated even when we eat, sleep, work and have fun is to be free of the bondage of extravagance, untroubled by whatever is and undisturbed by whatever isn't, delivered from lamentation about the past and hankering for the future. By remembering and applying His teachings, instead of relegating God to a small part of our life, we invite Him into every aspect of it. Such a mood is a fortress where contentment resides, liberated from the death knell of lethargy. Our attention shifts from worldly goals to the higher awareness that conducts our immediate activity. When our acts are truly worthy of us – when they benefit the *jivatma* – and when we do them in a worthy way – in accord with God's teachings – we're balanced.

This is the process of yoga known as bhakti, devotional service to God.

*We should therefore live in such a way that we keep ourselves always healthy and strong in mind and intelligence, so that we can distinguish the goal of life from a life full of problems.*

— Bhaktivedanta Swami Prabhupada

**Established in the self, one never departs from the truth, and upon gaining this one thinks there is no greater gain. Being situated in such a position, one is never shaken, even in the midst of the greatest difficulty. 6.22**

## The Glorious Self

God, the Supreme Person, has senses. Unlike our senses, however, His are unlimited. Wherever we go He's aware of our pleasures and pains, He hears our words, He sees what we're doing and He speaks to us through the scriptures.

In Bhagavad-gita God says, "Don't try to please your senses and mind, for that is futile. Try to please My senses and mind by engaging in bhakti, unmotivated and uninterrupted devotional service to Me." By guiding us away from matter and toward spirit, God re-establishes the dignity of each *jivatma*.

> An intelligent person does not take part in the sources of misery, which are due to contact with the material senses. Such pleasures have a beginning and an end, and so the wise person does not delight in them.
>
> — Bhagavad-gita 5.22

Bhakti will not exist just anywhere, but only with that person who has made some spiritual strides.

> In the minds of those who are too attached to sense enjoyment and material opulence, and who are bewildered by such things, the resolute determination for bhakti does not take place.
>
> — Bhagavad-gita 2.44

When I accept, even theoretically, that I am an integral component of God and can happily use my senses, mind and intelligence in His service, I begin to attract the supramundane power of bhakti. *Jivatma* is meant for bhakti; its search for happiness and harmony culminates in bhakti, and bhakti answers the call of its heart. At that time my senses, mind and intelligence, instead of subjugating me, come under my control. The shroud of ignorance dissipates.

> Bhakti, devotional service, dissolves the subtle body of the living entity without separate effort, just as fire in the stomach digests all that we eat.
>
> — Srimad-Bhagavatam 3.25.33

One winter, my husband's work took us on a five-month trip to Mumbai, India. Not long after we arrived, Priya, then eleven, became friends with two wonderful sisters with whom she played almost daily while she also took regular art, dance and tennis lessons, explored museums and planetariums, enjoyed boat rides and amusement parks, and dutifully continued her school work. But in spite of it all, Priya felt ill at ease and unsatisfied. Mumbai could never be her home. Just as our daughter longed for Sharanagati, so does the *jivatma* long for spiritual life, bhakti.

Each of us is immortal, wise and jubilant. In the inner recesses of our heart we know this with a certainty that needs no external proof. But as "modern people" we've largely lost faith in anything that science has not validated – often to our detriment. For example, we now know that despite propaganda to the contrary, chemical pesticides can cause more problems than they solve and that natural deterrents are far better. But our tendency is to let popular opinion, which is based on changing notions, predominate over our intuition and common sense.

Bhagavad-gita cuts through our waffling and reminds us to be what we already are: glorious, fulfilled spiritual beings who happily engage in bhakti, our constitutional activity.

> When the mind is restrained from material mental activities by practice of bhakti-yoga one can see the *jivatma* by the pure mind, and one relishes and rejoices in the *jivatma*. In that joyous state, one is situated in boundless transcendental happiness, realized through transcendental senses.
>
> — Bhagavad-gita 6.20–21

*Jivatma* is more than we could ever imagine it to be, yet it lives in a foreign land – this world of material objects and desires – and so is lost and lonely. Although *jivatma* feels estranged from its present situation, it has only a faint awareness of its own unique potential. In Sharanagati the hope of self-realization and harmony so fills us that we've pulled away from chasing mundane success and popularity. During moments of introspection, we've noted that the chase brings with it throes of vacancy and confusion.

*Jivatma's* nature is to enjoy, but it tries to enjoy through the material senses. True happiness is transcendental to those senses, and one who, by God's grace, attains that happiness does not need anything else. Once situated in bhakti yoga we think, "Oh, nothing is better than this!" After the beauty of bhakti has come into our life we understand why worldly enjoyments and attainments are flat and tasteless. I thought my first book would prove a great and satisfying accomplishment. It didn't. My perplexity persisted. Only when bhakti entered my life did meaning and purpose also enter; writing this book has been far more satisfying than the first one.

When we're inspired by bhakti, we're undisturbed even in great danger. We see everything that happens as God-arranged and are grateful for His miracles – the faint fragrance of a wild rose, the silkiness of its petals, their exquisite gradations from pink to white – small portals to the unsurpassed refinement of God's artistry.

*We were born to make manifest the glory of God that is within us. It's not just in some of us: it's in everyone. And as we let our own light shine, we unconsciously give other people permission to do the same.*

— Nelson Mandela

*The soul is a spiritual spark many, many times more illuminating, dazzling and powerful than the sun, moon or electricity. Human life is spoiled when people do not realize their real identity as soul.*

— Bhaktivedanta Swami Prabhupada

**For one who sees Me everywhere and sees everything in Me, I am never lost, nor is that person ever lost to Me. 6.30**

## Beautiful Vision

From the rocky outposts of the ridges to the thick sweep of firs on the mountainsides to the valley's flatlands laced by a brook and several lakes, God is present in Sharanagati as His encompassing energy. Remembering His presence shrinks personal problems and social discord to their true perspective just as, after a long mountain climb, we look down and are startled to see the home and garden where we toil daily become lost specks in a lush panorama. Everything material can potentially connect us to the immenseness of spirit.

> As long as we are in the material world, we are seated on the material energy, and therefore we are situated in Krishna, because Krishna's energy is not separate from Krishna ... Seeing Krishna everywhere means seeing every living being as well as everything else in relationship to Krishna.
>
> — Bhaktivedanta Swami Prabhupada

To become enchanted by this awareness is the adventure of God consciousness, a lifelong search for that elusive yet central Person from whom everything has come, in whom it exists and into whom it will one day enter; that singular Supreme Person who has the interests of each *jivatma* at heart.

> A person in Krishna consciousness certainly sees Krishna everywhere, and he sees everything in Krishna. Such a person may appear to see all separate manifestations of the material nature, but in each and every instance he is conscious of Krishna, knowing that everything is the manifestation of Krishna's energy. Nothing can exist without Krishna, and Krishna is the Lord of everything – this is the basic principle of Krishna consciousness.
>
> — Bhaktivedanta Swami Prabhupada

As a mother looking at her child's small shoes will see her child, so one who has abiding affection for God continually sees Him. The rest of us, who have not yet attained this love-imbued stage, can also see God always – through knowledge:

> How does the devotee know that everything is the manifestation of Krishna's energy? First of all, a Krishna conscious person is a philosopher. If he sees a tree, he thinks, "What is this tree?" He then sees that the tree's body is material energy, and the devotee automatically questions, "Whose energy? Krishna's

energy. Therefore the tree is connected to Krishna. Being a living entity, the tree is part and parcel of Krishna." In this way, the Krishna conscious person does not see the tree, but sees Krishna present.

— Bhaktivedanta Swami Prabhupada

Awareness of God is available even in a humble garden. I began my Sharanagati garden experience with stewardship. I cleared and leveled the land, thus giving our small parcel a more tamed beauty (as opposed to a wild beauty), and fenced it in to protect it. Although modest, my garden keeps me in touch with the earth and, through empathy with its goings-on, reminds me of my vulnerability and transience. My garden also keeps me and my family in the loop: in our home, nothing organic is thrown in the trash. It all goes into our compost pile, along with manure, hay, ashes and sawdust, then into the garden, where we're rewarded with dark, friable, fertile soil.

An added and unexpected benefit to this garden is the untold gratification we get from simply looking out our living and dining room windows to see our fruit trees – in spring, so laden with white flowers that they look snowed-on – and our lush vegetables. There is a certain nobility, a certain ineffable rightness to this view and to the roots we have set down in this remote corner of the earth. Here I feel closer to myself and to others. Just being in my tiny plot I feel harmony with the earth and her creatures. A garden nurtures relatedness and gratitude.

When I visit my city friends and see organic matter – fruit peel, vegetable parts, leftovers – in the trash, I have an urge to gather it all up and ship it to Sharanagati. Meanwhile, what my city friends eat is often grown by far-away farmers who use harmful chemical fertilizers instead of trashed organic matter. An ugly anomaly lurks in this scenario.

Why not live a simple, healthy, largely stress-free life among fellow spiritual seekers? Why not appreciate the earth and her many creatures? Why not come closer to God, the Supreme Father? Just gardening for Him can enrich us beyond our expectations. In my decades of urban and suburban living I never found the security and empowerment I feel in Sharanagati – independence from humankind's stress-filled economic system, dependence on providence and, by taking God's words to heart, a sense that I'm in touch with the pulse of wholeness.

*The Godhead is so mystically creative, cleverly subtle and extraordinarily diverse that recognizing and honoring Him at every moment requires great mindfulness. In other words, mindfulness means to constantly see Krishna or God in everything at all times. It involves the recognition of God's right to be what He wants, when He wants, and interact with us as He likes.*

— Bhakti Tirtha Swami

**One is a perfect yogi who, by comparison to one's own self, sees the true equality of all beings, in both their happiness and their distress. 6.32**

## Compassion

> Thou shalt love thy neighbor as thyself.
>
> — The Ten Commandments

That "self" is a *jivatma* incarcerated by a material body and mind. Compassion is to help free that self from its awkward circumstance.

To have compassion for another *jivatma*, regardless of its body, is a normal quality for a civilized person. Based on our spiritual identity, *jivatma*, and based on our material predicament – our body is mortal and subject to all sorts of suffering – we have a kindred spirit with all beings.

Compassion that ignores the *jivatma* and concerns itself only with the body is not approved by Krishna.

> Seeing Arjuna full of compassion, his mind depressed, his eyes full of tears, Krishna spoke the following words. "My dear Arjuna, how has this bodily concept of life come upon you? It is not at all befitting a person who knows the value of life. It leads not to elevation but to degradation."
>
> — Bhagavad-gita 2.1–2

As I play my role in the web of life, Bhagavad-gita's view of compassion makes me aware of my spiritual kinship with fellow creatures and inspires my sensitivity. Chanakya Pandit, a scholar and moralist in the fourth century B.C., said:

> An educated man sees all women except his wife as his mother, and an educated woman sees all men except her husband as her son; they see others' property as garbage in the street; and they look on the sufferings of others as if they themselves were suffering the same pain.

Learned persons (whether or not they have prestigious titles) are not unlawfully lusty or greedy and are compassionate: they treat others as

they want to be treated. If something would pain me, I wouldn't inflict it on others – including animals. In Bhaktivedanta Swami's words,

> If your throat is cut, if your head is cut, you feel so much pain, so how can you cut the head of an animal? This is education ... One should not think that since the spirit spark is never killed even after the body dies then there is no harm in killing animals for

> sense gratification. People are now addicted to eating animals, in spite of having an ample supply of grains, fruits and milk. There is no necessity for animal killing. This injunction is for everyone.

Like millions of people throughout the world, all the residents of Sharanagati, including my family and me, are vegetarian. We don't eat meat, fish or eggs. Typical (yet now old-fashioned) responses to this are,

"But what do you eat?"

"How do you get enough protein?"

I became a vegetarian at age twenty when I first went to India and discovered literally hundreds of dishes, most of them delicious, that not only satisfied me but also left me feeling stronger yet lighter than my former non-vegetarian diet had. In traditional Indian cooking, milk, yogurt, butter or cheese form the basis of dozens of marvels and, along with many types of legume dishes, thoroughly answer the protein question. I have never regretted my vegetarian choice – in fact, I sometimes look back on my non-vegetarian decades and feel disappointed in myself: for far too long I was blind to the animals' suffering and the many ills of meat-eating.

Some Sharanagati residents are excellent cooks, and each day in each home they make a variety of healthy, palatable, satisfying vegetarian dishes for family meals. On festival days, which occur at least weekly, we all come together in the main temple, offer our homemade dishes to God and then happily share those dishes with each other in a grand community potluck feast. Effortlessly, joyfully, we spare the lives of innocent animals and in the process protect and enhance our health, do our bit for the earth's ecological balance and are re-spiritualized.

> If one offers Me with love and devotion a leaf, a flower, fruit or water, I will accept it.
>
> — Bhagavad-gita 9.26, Krishna speaking

By instinct animals kill to survive. But we humans can be healthy – healthier, actually – without killing animals for food. Indifference to others' suffering, including the suffering of lower species, is unconscionable. A steely, profit-driven, me-first, I-want-it-now culture proliferates such indifference and creates an emptiness and a gnawing coldness within us. Indifference destroys our world's natural harmony. As we deplete the earth and are cruel to her creatures, so we deplete ourselves and mutilate our own hearts.

We can lessen our contribution to the world's spiraling crises of over-consumption, pollution, confusion, crime, war, stress, disease and meaninglessness. We can care about how our acts affect the planet and the creatures on it, whether those acts relate to using toxic chemicals in our kitchen sink or to the destruction of a rain forest several continents away or to the needless slaughter of animals. And we can bear with fate's alarming vicissitudes.

Once my neighbor Gisele and her family left Sharanagati for a week and invited a friend from the city to stay in their house at that time. Before the friend left their home, she closed all the doors and windows of the house save one that she didn't notice. When Gisele returned a few days later, her nine-year old daughter went into the house first and then ran out.

"Mom! There's a bear in the house!"

It was dusk and Gisele, who was unpacking the car and who'd been driving all day, said, "I'm too tired for jokes. Let's get inside."

"No, no, it's true. There's a bear inside!"

Gisele peered in through her front window to see a 400-pound bear, which had entered through the open side window, emptying her kitchen cabinets in search of food. Gisele ran around and opened her side doors wide, then returned to the front door and, along with her daughter, made a great hubbub by calling out, banging and stomping.

The bear, disturbed, grumbled and sauntered out the side door, leaving a complete mess behind.

The connection we share with all that lives, including intruding bears, begins with our common spiritual identity. It then expands to include the material body of the *jivatma* and goes on expanding to include the planet we share. Through knowledge and the compassion it brings we're mystically enriched by an ethos of generosity that transcends our species.

And compassion includes forgiving and tolerating our own foibles, for as the Commandment says, we can only be as loving to others as we are to ourselves.

It also includes forgiving the foibles of hungry bears.

*How can one who harms others attain happiness?*

— Srimad-Bhagavatam 10.44.47

**A transcendentalist engaged in auspicious activities does not meet with destruction either in this world or in the spiritual world; one who does good is never overcome by evil. 6.40**

## Faith

Like the families of swans that rest on Lake Sharanagati each fall and use it as a guide-point for their migration south, we residents of Sharanagati rest on the waters of faith in God and guru.

> Only unto those great souls who have implicit faith in both God and the spiritual master are all the imports of the scriptures automatically revealed.
>
> — Svetasvatara Upanisad 6.23

Faith – unflinching trust in the sublime – is intrinsic to the *jivatma* and is meant for God and the guru. If we do not place our faith there, in transcendence, our faith will repose in something lesser, something disappointing, where it will be battered by doubt and languish dispiritedly. As we reduce the object of our faith to something less than it was meant for, something less than sublime, we reduce both our faith

and ourselves. We wallow in the commonplace. Even more, ill-placed faith produces ill-fated results.

> Those who say there is no God in control, who are lost to themselves and who have no intelligence, engage in unbeneficial, horrible works meant to destroy the world.
>
> — Bhagavad-gita 16.9

God does not give Himself cheaply. Beyond the range of our mind and intelligence and sense perception, beyond all the godlessness of this world, covered by the curtain of His own deluding energy, God, who is unseen and unheard yet around us all the time, tests our faith. Bhaktivedanta Swami Prabhupada writes, "The material energy is always provoking doubts about the supreme authority of God."

How to give up doubts? By humbly placing them before our spiritual mentor, as Arjuna did, and hearing from that person.

> O Krishna, I ask You to dispel my doubts completely. But for You, no one is to be found who can destroy these doubts.
>
> — Bhagavad-gita 6.39

Through hearing we learn of God's greatness and awaken to the flavor of His plan.

> Religion without philosophy is sentiment, or sometimes fanaticism, while philosophy without religion is mental speculation.
>
> — Bhaktivedanta Swami Prabhupada

Once I'd accepted theism to be more reasonable than atheism then, although my moods would change, faith let me continue to hear and apply Bhaktivedanta Swami Prabhupada's teachings. Their impact amazed me.

> If you are indeed interested in logic and argument, kindly apply it to the mercy of God. If you do so, you will find it to be strikingly wonderful.
>
> — Chaitanya Charitamrita 1.8.15

My morsel of faith in God inspired me to become worthy of God's trust, to try to improve myself and to keep company with people of the same bent.

Here in Sharanagati we residents do not pretend to have more faith than we do. We do not pretend to have realized our intimate relationship with God or to be overwhelmed with love for Him, for pretense does not honor Him. We simply hold a hope of being spiritually nourished by our faith in Him, in our spiritual teacher, in the scriptures and in each other. Faith is our individual voluntary desire to do His will and to become worthy of His faith in us.

Many of my neighbors chose Sharanagati and Bhagavad-gita because they grew tired of religions that did nothing to change their view of reality, which did not lessen their anxieties and illusions, which left them prey to upheavals, which lacked coherence. In making our choices, my neighbors and I are aware that only firm faith can bring us to God, and that without faith other qualities – leadership, eloquence, expertise – lack spiritual value. But if, in the future, all the wealth of our experience betrays us and we naively trust someone who proves untrustworthy, we pray that faith will enable us to place our disappointment and pain before God and allow us to remain spiritually hopeful and free of cynicism. If we have just a grain of faith left, we will offer it to God, for that single grain is more valuable than tons of faithlessness.

Faith is knowing my identity as a tiny part of God and recognizing my insignificance before Him. Faith is realizing that God is with me and enthusiastically and patiently engaging in bhakti, service to Him. Faith allows me to live by it even when it offers me no consolation.

Faith is confidence in my potential to commune with that personal God of spacious grace who is the source of all that is permanent and all that is temporary. Faith without pride bridges the chasm between what I am and what I ought to be. Faith is accompanied by self-realization and a reverent appreciation of everyday life. Faith inspires courage in devotion.

Faith is granted to those who earnestly desire it and who seek the company of those who have it. It is not acceptance without proof; it is my instinctive migration toward my original position. Faith is an unobstructed perception of the unseen. It's the invisible guide that transports the swans to their rightful home.

*Those who follow this imperishable path of devotional service and who completely engage themselves with faith, making Me the supreme goal, are very, very dear to Me.*

— Bhagavad-gita 12.20, Krishna speaking

*Let me face the future unafraid.*
*Today is good: to-morrow taunts with fear.*
*To-morrow I shall find but God's to-day*
*To prove anew His presence near.*

— William Massie

*If ye have faith as a grain of mustard seed ... nothing shall be impossible unto you.*

— Matthew 17:20

*God did not call me to be successful; He called me to be faithful.*

— Mother Teresa

**As pearls are strung on a thread so everything rests upon Me. 7.7**

## Abundance

If all that exists are pearls, God is their supporting thread.

Some of Sharanagati's pearls are peace, simplicity, ample space, good friends, convivial devotional service to God and, most importantly, lasting gratitude for it all. The gracious and loyal companion of such gratitude is a sense of abundance: a feeling of overflowing fullness not from proprietorship, but from happiness.

> One who seeks pleasure externally is a materialist, and one who seeks pleasure internally is a spiritualist.
>
> — Bhaktivedanta Swami Prabhupada

In every other place my family and I have lived we've had many more neighbors than we do now, but we didn't appreciate them as much or feel as gratified by their company as we do now. Also, in other places we used much more; now the attic of our rustic little Sharanagati home is filled with rows of boxes of no-longer-needed clothes, books, toys, equipment, papers, utensils and machines. How little one actually needs! And how rich we become by appreciating what we have and by using it as it is meant to be used. In the furor to own more one becomes a pauper despite plenitude, suffocated by the superfluous.

Bhagavad-gita frees us from unnecessary wants, from neediness that is not based on need, from a poverty of appreciation.

> A person who is not disturbed by the incessant flow of desires that enter like rivers into the ocean – which is ever being filled but is always still – can alone achieve peace, and not the man who strives to satisfy such desires.
>
> — Bhagavad-gita 2.70

Bhagavad-gita establishes a culture of abundance so deep that even in the center of a city, with its bustling minute-by-minute demands and its pressure to perform, one can still feel grateful. The Gita calms the whirlwind of passion that pushes us to get things rather than to appreciate them, to exploit beauty and power rather than to honor them, and to acquire knowledge for prestige and remuneration rather than its life-changing revelations.

> Everything animate or inanimate that is within the universe is controlled and owned by God. One should therefore accept only

> those things necessary for oneself, which are set aside as one's quota, and one should not accept other things, knowing well to whom they belong.
>
> — Sri Isopanisad Mantra 1

We don't actually possess anything; for a short time we simply steward some things that are owned by God. Abundance means to reconnect those things – a rose or a business venture, land or a home, our life energy or the government of a country – to their owner.

When I try to use possessions, abilities and work for my own pleasure I experience scarcity. Counterintuitively, hedonism does not bring lasting happiness, because it's based on the false premise that my own pleasure is life's highest goal, which it isn't. The pearl necklace my husband placed around my neck some years ago was elegant, and I admired it and relished the love behind it, but without the thread that holds those pearls together there would be no necklace, no elegance and no relishing. To remember the hidden thread behind all possessions, abilities and work is to remember God. His hidden support is imbued with His love for us. And His pleasure is the source of our mysterious sense of abundance.

Abundance means to use things wisely, to get full value from life not through conquest, status, success and achievement, but by seeing everything as God's rather than mine or anyone else's. When we use an item remembering its actual owner and in the way He wants it used, we're in touch with abundance. When we find time to care for the details of our surroundings and for the people in our life, we're in touch with abundance. If nothing seems sacred and no one cares, appreciation shrivels and we become distant, cold, hard. When a house in Sharanagati is neglected, with a tangle of weeds outside and dirty inside, it means either the owners have moved away or – worse – they've stopped caring.

Abundance is to make more available for others by learning to flourish in that elusive state of "enough." It's being efficient at reaping God consciousness in a world filled with distraction. Abundance is the elegant use of money, time, energy, space and possessions. It's when one finds the devotional opportunity tucked inside each time, place and circumstance.

Just a hint of God's fullness and generosity is an abundance that uplifts our hearts; we greet each morning with eagerness. Life is precious.

Strung on the thread of faith and decorated with pearls of abundance, a garland of harmony encircles those fortunate *jivatmas* who sincerely serve the Lord and His creation.

*All these cities and villages are flourishing in all respects because the herbs and grains are in abundance, the trees are full of fruits, the rivers are flowing, the hills are full of minerals and the oceans full of wealth. And this is all due to Your glancing over them.*

— Srimad-Bhagavatam 1.8.40, Queen Kunti speaking to Krishna

**Action pertaining to the development of the material bodies of the living entities is called karma. 8.3**

## Karma

Our land, couched by tens of thousands of forested mountains, is slowly and endlessly shaped by nature's laws. Although we cannot always understand why the land is the way it is, from the 6,680-foot-high peak in the north to the trace minerals in our garden loam, some cause is behind every aspect of it. And each cause creates an effect. Blueberries don't grow well here as we have a dry climate and alkaline soil; raspberries, however, thrive. Our world is governed by cause and effect, action and reaction, law and order.

Karma is a law that works on the subtle, human plane and is perceived through reasoning. The human freedom to choose what we do makes us responsible for our choices; and the reactions to our actions are karma, the effects or "fruits" of our choices. These fruits appear in our life as events that are good, bad or mixed and that give us varieties of pleasures or pains. Our past actions created our present situation and our current actions form our future situations. We may escape the government's laws, but we can no sooner escape the laws of karma than the force of gravity. Karma unerringly brings each of us what we deserve.

So the circumstances in which we currently find ourselves are not flukes but are connected to our past as much as fertilizing the soil is connected to the quality of the future crop. We benefit from our honorable desires and acts, we suffer from our vices, and the witness of it all is our inner friend and guide, Paramatma.

> God is the constant companion of the living entity as Paramatma, or the Supersoul, and therefore He can understand the desires of

> the individual soul, as one can smell the flavor of a flower by being near it ... and the Lord, being neutral to everyone, does not interfere with the desires of the minute independent living entities.
>
> — Bhaktivedanta Swami Prabhupada

In all forms of life, death is not the cessation of the *jivatma's* existence, as the *jivatma* is eternal. Death means that the *jivatma* has left the body it was inhabiting, and conception means that the *jivatma* has entered another body appropriate to what it deserves.

> The perishable body embraces the *jivatma* and then leaves it aside.
>
> — Srimad-Bhagavatam 7.7.43

Thus the *jivatma* transmigrates from one body to another through various forms – fish, plant, bird, animal – and when it comes to the human form it may finally ask, "Why am I suffering?" Only in the human form does the living entity accrue karma and is caught in a continuum of desire, action and reaction. Without understanding reincarnation and the law of karma, happiness and distress appear haphazardly strewn amongst us without justification or predictability, like fallen leaves scattered by a gust of wind. Together, reincarnation and karma allow us to reasonably resolve the enigma of our fortune and misfortune. They tell me why I am in my particular body looking at the world through particularly nearsighted eyes, and why learning to swim was for me a near-effortless joy while learning chemistry was Sisyphean.

By understanding the cycle of karma I can also learn how to end it.

> We are suffering or enjoying the results of our activities from time immemorial, but we can change the results of our karma, or our activity, and this change depends on the perfection of our knowledge.
>
> — Bhaktivedanta Swami Prabhupada

"The perfection of our knowledge" does not necessarily mean that we must become perfect in mind, word and action, but that we gain a heartfelt loyalty to God and His purpose.

> An ordinary person with firm faith in the eternal injunctions of God, even though unable to execute such orders, becomes liberated from the bondage of the law of karma.
>
> — Bhaktivedanta Swami Prabhupada

As a sparrow uses aerodynamics to defy gravity, so by knowledge of and faith in God's directives we can become free from the grip of karma.

With knowledge and faith we take responsibility for our present difficulties and trials, for they are due to our own previous inappropriate actions. This does not absolve the guilt of those who have harmed us – they will suffer for their acts – but knowing our responsibility in the matter can help dissolve our rage toward them. An understanding of karma and reincarnation awakens us to a great plan, and accepting these principles establishes us in mindful thoughts – thoughts not created out of envy or anger, hankering or lamenting, greed or bitterness – as well as

in mindful words and mindful actions. Rather than being resigned to fate, we experience it as an observer who has resolved to put an end to it.

> Even if one is liberated, he nevertheless accepts the body he has received according to his past karma. Without misconceptions, however, he regards his enjoyment and suffering due to that karma the way an awakened person regards a dream he had while sleeping. He thus remains steadfast and never works to achieve another material body.
>
> — Srimad-Bhagavatam 5.1.16

Counterarguments to karma, like the idea of happenstance, are neither reasonable nor logical. And the concept of an ineffective, weak or uninvolved God who cannot or will not stop our suffering contradicts the very definition of God as all-good and all-powerful. Knowledge of karma frees the *jivatma* from the confused dream known as life in the material world.

*God is not responsible for the* jivatma's *accepting different types of bodies. One has to accept a body according the laws of nature and one's own karma.*

— Bhaktivedanta Swami Prabhupada

*Don't complain. What you got is what you earned in your previous life.*

— The Tao

*No matter how much parents and grandparents may have sinned against the child, the man who is really adult will accept these sins as his own condition which has to be reckoned with. Only a fool is interested in other people's guilt, since he cannot alter it. The wise man learns only from his own guilt. He will ask himself: who am I that all this should happen to me? To find the answer to that fateful question he will look into his own heart.*

— C. G. Jung

*I believe in the golden rule – do good things and good things will happen to you.*

— Cesar Millan

3

# Harmony with Others

*As we continue our pilgrimage our path broadens and we are challenged to create harmony within our many and diverse relationships. Bhagavad-gita explains that the* jivatma *is enlivened and fulfilled by bhakti – by selfless and caring service to God and to every aspect of His creation, including the various people in our lives. Bhakti is our deepest feeling and activity, and it arouses a genuine commonality with all types of individuals, even those markedly difficult or different. With grace – the favor of one greater than us – bhakti enables our relationships to overcome obstacles and even to thrive despite them; pure bhakti, the epitome of intimacy, transcends all barriers. Each and every one of us is an integral part of God and each and every one of us is attracted to and beautified by bhakti, the sublime relationship harmonizer.*

**Krishna said: Because you are never envious of Me, I shall impart to you this most confidential knowledge and realization, knowing which you shall be relieved of the miseries of material existence. 9.1**

## Freedom from Envy

Olga, my Russian-born friend and neighbor in Sharanagati, gave me Chinese lantern roots for my garden. With happy thoughts of their dried pumpkin-colored pods dangling from our winter vases, I didn't pay much attention when she said, "Watch out, they take over." Two years later, Chinese lanterns had invaded the entirety of my large circular bed, crowding my herbs, berries and vegetables.

"Why did I get myself into this?" I cried.

"How did I forget Olga's warning?" I lamented.

Then I became grim: "I will fight until the last root is out."

On my knees, waving off mosquitoes, I spent weeks digging up thick, cream-colored lantern roots that crisscrossed the garden like a subway system and burrowed sixteen inches down. Occasionally, John and Priya would watch from our front porch and ponder my sanity.

Like Chinese lanterns in my Canadian garden, envy is foreign to me – a *jivatma* – but it invades my heart along with material desires and attachments. Another person's success, advantages or possessions become the dangling baubles that I covet for the vase of my glum life. Bhaktivinode Thakur, speaking on behalf of our lower nature, writes, "Perpetually speaking lies, I become dejected upon seeing others happy, whereas the misery of others is a source of great delight for me."

Arjuna's singular qualification for hearing Bhagavad-gita is that he is free of the degrading emotion of envy. He neither competes with God nor thinks that he is God nor that he can become God. I may think,

"Well, I don't envy God, I just envy so-and-so, who is more accomplished and popular than I." But ultimately, to envy anyone for anything is to envy God, for that person's attributes are God's gift to them in the form of their good karma. My life is not meant to be weed-infested but a bouquet of happiness. What can I do?

I can get down very low and follow the stem down through the dark soil to its root, uncover and tug at the root until it's free and then expose it to the withering sunlight. I cannot resent the time, the effort, the determination, the vastness of this project. I simply make a commitment and act on it regularly.

Roots produce stems; mundane desires and attachments produce envy. When, by spiritual knowledge, I am convinced that nothing of this material world will last, I unearth mundane desires and, under the light of detachment, they perish.

In gardening, as in life, one has to keep at it: observing, learning, weeding, planting, watering and assisting nature's way. My fierce attack on Chinese lanterns that summer gave the strawberries, echinacea and yellow squash that were already in the garden more space, just as uprooting envy allows my innate God-given qualities to flourish.

To be free from envy I need the humility to accept my lot in life, the contentment to avoid comparing myself with others, and the gift of absorption in whatever service I do for God's pleasure. To be deeply absorbed in a service is to feel my uniqueness, for as God is extraordinarily unique, in a tiny but complete way I am also unique. I am a small gardener among numerous other gardeners, I have a small role that contributes to the vast garden, and I can perform that role with joy. I need not begrudge or thwart the roles of others, but I enhance those roles with my own, as they enhance mine. I appreciate another's possessions or abilities for I see in them the design of God. I appreciate the goodness in others and am happy for their success, knowing that they are, as I am, a unique and integral part of the same God. By seeing another with a little love and devotion, my heart becomes cleansed of envy. Finally, when I am sincerely able to serve the same person I formerly envied, the harvest of my heart is healthy.

The appearance of envy means I've neglected my identity and my role in God's creation. It indicates that my knowledge is incomplete and that I'm untrue to myself. It means I think something in this mundane world will bring me happiness. It means weeds are choking out succulent vegetables. Envy is a loss of perspective: I forget it's another person's time for success; I forget that my success is in living in the moment with moment-to-moment mindfulness of God. Sometime, whether in this lifetime or the next, that mindfulness will come.

To envy anything material, including another's wealth, good health, intelligence, fame or talent, is unworthy of me. What I have is not an accident, for there aren't any accidents; there is only karma, which is based on universal laws, and God's causeless grace. By His grace seeds fructify into nourishing plants and I become fortunate enough to sincerely desire another's enduring spiritual and material success.

*True peace dwells only in the heart of the humble: but the heart of the proud is ever full of pride and jealousy.*

— Thomas à Kempis

*Don't be jealous. Others have only what fate has given them.*

— Confucius

*God alone can sound the heart! How shortsighted His creatures can be! They find a soul whose lights surpass their own; they think the Lord loves them less. Yet when did He lose the right to use one of His children to provide others with the nourishment they need?*

— St. Therese of Lisieux

*In the material world, when someone surpasses us in some way we become angry and plan how to stop him, but in the spiritual world when someone does some better service we think "Oh, he has done so nicely. Let me help him to execute his service." So we should always endeavor to keep this attitude, and serve Krishna to the best of our ability. That will make one advance in spiritual life.*

— Bhaktivedanta Swami Prabhupada

**Those who are not deluded, the great souls, are under the protection of the divine nature. They are fully engaged in devotional service because they know God, who is original and inexhaustible. 9.13**

## Good Company

We residents of Sharanagati have a common and lifelong purpose, a purpose that, like our creek, circumvents obstacles to wend through, sustain and beautify our valley.

Here, perspectives change. Here, no one is obliged to rush; no one has to pretend to sparkle. Individuals are accepted for being just what they are – aspiring devotees of God. How full, how good, how less stressful life is when we live with diverse yet like-minded people, where each person stands for nothing but himself or herself, where the qualifications we lack don't disqualify us, where those notes we sing off-key and our out-of-fashion pants and our faux pas aren't so embarrassing – where stature is based on the privilege equally available to each individual: the sincere attempt to please guru and God by following their directives.

Good company rids one of greed and faithlessness, confused thoughts and weakness of heart. Through fellowship with those who want to mature spiritually, our enthusiasm for selfless unmotivated service to God grows. We become confident of the path and pursue it with patience.

Time, however, tests commitments. In Sharanagati we have fought forest fires and philosophical challenges equally. We have read, argued, prayed, played, cooked, laughed, learned and built homes together. We have danced and sung, partied and paraded, and shared losses and accomplishments. Through it all we remain united in the common endeavor to come closer to God.

The passing years have turned our admiration for, and reliance on, our neighbors into abiding affection. Yet this is not a closed or elite group: our circle gladly enlarges to include more kindred souls, each valued, each with his or her unique aspects to add.

On a larger scale, perhaps it will become widely known that the qualities of the *jivatma* – resolution, integrity, compassion, and especially faith – are best nourished in a devotional community. Perhaps the children of settled families in such communities will also decide to

live there and allow their parents' experience to inform and guide their actions. Perhaps, through the spiritual strength that good company offers, individuals, each in their own way, will gradually overcome God's deluding power.

In the end, good company is the real opulence and wonder any place has to offer.

*Without good association, one cannot achieve transcendental knowledge.*

— Bhaktivedanta Swami Prabhupada

*If we really want to effectively associate with others, we really have to learn how to develop the ability to see the good qualities in others. If we really want to develop the ability to see the good qualities in others, we really have to look within our own hearts to see the unwanted things that are obstructing us and preventing us from seeing.*

— Niranjana Swami

*Just be yourself. Everyone else is taken.*

— Message in a greeting card

**Those who always worship Me, meditating on My transcendental form – to them I carry what they lack, and I preserve what they have. 9.22**

## Our Sustenance

God is present in the morning sunlight that pokes through the leaves of my young apple tree. He is present in the hearts of my family and friends, and He is present in those persons who wish me ill. It's easier to feel God's presence in some places or people – like a temple or a friend – than others – like the compost pile or a critic. But in fact He is present everywhere.

> When God is pleased with the living entity because of one's devotional service, that person becomes learned and does not distinguish between enemies, friends and oneself. Intelligently, that person thinks, "Every one of us is an eternal servant of God, and therefore we are not different from one another."
>
> — Srimad-Bhagavatam 7.5.12

Devotional service, done with trust and without demanding a particular outcome, transforms the servants: with humility and grace they discern between favorable and unfavorable acts, they do their best, and they see God in all that happens and in all relationships.

> Discretion is the better part of valor, and one must learn how to discriminate between actions which may be pleasing to God and those which may not be pleasing to God. An action is thus judged by God's pleasure or displeasure. There is no room for personal whims; we must always be guided by the pleasure of God.
>
> — Bhaktivedanta Swami Prabhupada

Sometimes, dense with opinion, I harden around a position, demanding to be right, to win and to establish myself. My stubborn self-seeking creates strained exchanges and hurts those close to me. I forget who I am, my actual self-interest and duty and how to interact with others. When a lumber company proposed to selectively thin our Sharanagati forests in exchange for the wood they cut, I supported the idea thinking less-crowded forests would be healthier and have less forest fire risk. The majority of community members, however, were against the proposal, seeing it as complicating our lives and sensing that the lumberjacks would leave an ugly footprint with their cuttings and new forest roadways. Looking back, I agree with the majority and realize that I spoke when I should have listened; I was fixed when I should have been flexible. Unnecessarily, I'd damaged bonds, and I apologized and made amends.

As God is the well-wisher of each of us, so are His servants. In the presence of such well-wishers ordinary relationships become extraordinary. What I lack is compensated for, and what I have is preserved. More, when I'm in the presence of well-wishers, I become like them – a well-wisher. Listening to and confiding in one another we become stronger and, on conferring, together we detect in a surprising number of our neighbors some unique combination of honesty, intelligence, munificence, conviction and sagacity. Appreciation for them sustains us.

In God, the master of all mystics, contradictions are reconciled and conflicts concluded. Although I am shallow, I can have faith in His depth and breadth. He can lift me from the quicksand of false arguments and the firestorms of unfortunate situations. He can dispel my pettiness, clarify my life and inspire good, simple, heartfelt dealings. By His mercy I can be close to those who are spiritually inclined, respect but remain aloof from antagonistic people, and become focused on the reality that all life is sacred because every *jivatma* is divine. Friends and enemies both are eternal servants of God and are therefore equal, but for me to realize their identity and equality I need the sustenance of good company. So I honor one and all, yet become close with fellow travelers on the spiritual path.

*Whatever appears to be of any value, if it is without relation to Me, has no reality. Know it as My illusory energy, that reflection which appears to be in darkness.*

— Srimad-Bhagavatam 2.9.34, Krishna speaking

*God makes the sun rise on the evil and on the good, and sends rain on the righteous and on the unrighteous.*

— Matthew 5:45

*Lord, within thy fold I be,*
*And I'm content;*
*Naught can be amiss to me,*
*For thy helping hand I see,*
*Light'ning loads that heavy be;*
*And I'm content.*

— Priscilla Jane Thompson

**Forgiveness, truthfulness, control of the senses, control of the mind – these various qualities of living beings are created by Me alone. 10.4**

## Forgiveness

Even though Sharanagati is a relatively small place with a small population that's united by common ideals, we, its residents, have seen marriages dissolve, friendships sour and parents grieve over their teenagers' choices. That another can hurt us is a sign of our humanness. How we react to that hurt, however deep and painful, rests in our humanity. While fortitude lets us endure the pain of a frigid winter or a bad fall, the pain caused by another, especially a friend or a relative, may undo us.

> If one is hurt by the arrows of an enemy, one is not as aggrieved as when cut by the unkind words of a relative, for such grief continues to rend one's heart day and night.
>
> — Srimad-Bhagavatam 4.3.19

At every moment I'm vulnerable to the miseries created by fate and by other people. Just as I cannot control providential misery, which awakens me to my helplessness and dependence, so I cannot control the words and actions of others. Harm from immoral and unethical behavior, from the weakness, witlessness and evil of another person, calls me to control my wrath and desire for revenge. By identifying the hurtful actions, by understanding how and why they are hurtful, and especially by regaining my sense of self, I can choose to forgive even a terrible injury. Instead of letting rage poison me, through forgiveness I can transform it: I can use it to educate and heal injurers. And through forgiveness I can heal myself.

I can also choose not to forgive, to hang on to grievance and grief and to remain stuck in blame, self-pity and resentment. Unforgiveness, even when caused by intense pain, continues my misery, burning my heart and crippling my mind. Once I've been hurt, the only way I, the victim, can undo the emotional damage is to forgive when I am ready. Forgiveness is a journey I take alone – no one else can forgive for me – that will restore me to normality. By forgiving I give myself the incomparable gift of freedom from anguish and, along with it, the ability to be happy again. Forgiveness, an ethical reaction to injury, in no way condones the injurers or lessens their due punishment, but it enables me, the injured, to return to the present, to here and now. The more painful the injury, the more strength I will need to forgive. But when I seek it, that strength is offered by God.

> God is so kind to His devotee that when severely testing him God gives him the necessary strength to be tolerant.
>
> — Bhaktivedanta Swami Prabhupada

The courage to tolerate and forgive, to break the shackles of negativity, comes from the Paramatma, the Supersoul. God doesn't want me to become stagnated by the past or to live in the grip of pain and hatred. Whatever else I may lose, I will always retain the possibility of hearing God's will. He, as my conscience, tells me to accept what is favorable for my well-being and to reject what is unfavorable. My freedom to be positive regardless of circumstances is a freedom that cannot be taken from me. It's always mine. I need only to decide to take it.

The *jivatma* wants to reside in a body blessed with a clear mind and a peaceful heart. It wants to forgive others for their transgressions and become once again responsible for its own happiness and future through service to God, His creation and His created beings.

John and I were traveling overseas with our daughter when a friend of hers invited her to sleep over. That night in her friend's house our daughter was inapppropriately approached by her friend's father, a divorcé who was a "friend" of ours. To get away from him, our daughter locked herself in the bathroom for hours. Months later she finally told us what had happened; John and I were appalled and furious. Our feelings didn't abate when this "friend" called. He spoke with me.

"Hey, listen, I'm so sorry about what happened."

"Yeah, you're sorry now that we've found out about it. How could you attack a young, helpless girl? How could you?"

"No, no, honestly. I don't know what came over me that night. It never happened before."

"Like hell it hasn't. Making a pass at an 11-year-old girl in the middle of the night doesn't come from nowhere. I'm worried about what you've done to your own daughter."

"Nothing! My daughter's fine! Don't accuse me! I'm sorry! I'm sorry!"

Eventually, John and I realized that we couldn't change what this person had done. But we could try to protect his daughter and other potential victims; we could help our daughter deal with the incident; and, although it was difficult, we could give up our fury. We reported this "friend's" behavior and much later forgave him.

Forgiveness is to give up all hope of changing the past. It's a process of expressing what happened, accepting it, acknowledging one's feelings, slowly healing and finally letting the past go.

The minute-by-minute possibility of some sort of harm in this world is not the random result of what appears to be mindless laws of nature. Life has meaning and purpose, and suffering, which is inherent to material life, also has meaning and purpose. Through suffering I may realize the necessity of positive beliefs and solid values. Or new people may enter my life to help me. Or I may learn to help others. God's mysterious and inscrutable plan is beyond my understanding, but even in suffering His orderly principle is at work.

The soundness of our character is tested by our capacity to forgive the suffering others impose on us. Those who meet life's ongoing quandaries with a wholesome understanding, with forgiveness, become better instead of bitter. This world's dark and unfathomable complexities and pains are lightened and eased by the life-enriching happiness that accompanies forgiveness. Those who truly forgive give affection without effort and receive it with joy. Theirs is a future opulent in heartfelt reciprocation.

*Nothing real can be threatened. Nothing unreal exists. Herein lies the peace of God.*

— *A Course in Miracles*

*Even the helpless victim of a hopeless situation, facing a fate he cannot change, may rise above himself, may grow beyond himself, and by doing so change himself. He may turn a personal tragedy into a triumph.*

— Victor Frankl

*God is pleased with those who are forgiving.*

— Srimad-Bhagavatam 9.15.40

**To those who are constantly devoted to serving Me with love, I give the understanding by which they can come to Me. 10.10**

## Standing Under

To forgive and to see calamity in perspective we need a certain openness, a softness and broadness of heart. What better place to unearth such vulnerability than in a small village cradled between expansive ranges of green mountains under a vast brilliant sky? Here, protected, we can peel away our cravings and stresses, our suspicions and toughness, and come closer to what we are: generous, friendly, jolly people. In Sharanagati the self is almost tangible.

Like the warm spring winds that make the wild flax dance, clear consciousness brings with it a revitalized and good life. This life comes not from lofty words or by a sharp wit or by earning lots of money, but simply by following the guidance of a genuine spiritual teacher. Although he passed away many years ago, my teacher, Bhaktivedanta Swami Prabhupada, is still present in my life through his teachings, his lifelong example and his love for me, an insignificant student. And although it may not be rational, somehow I feel that I remain in his life.

Informed of the transcendent realm by this teacher, we Sharanagati-ites have felt our horizons broaden, our lingering worldly preoccupations lessen and our desire for inner life stir. Since I see my neighbors bound by the same love of clear consciousness, I usually manage to subdue my critical, fault-finding nature and be humbled by their sincerity; I'm lucky to be among them.

It's rare for Westerners to live in a remote "off the grid" area that's patrolled by bears, plagued by mosquitoes and grasshoppers and subject to climatic extremes. Yet, my neighbors, my family and I are here and, in His kindness, God reveals to each willing heart the goodness of the other hearts. Guru and God open our eyes to the worthiness of our fellows, and as we perceive grace in the lives of our fellows our own bond with guru and God is fortified. We want to serve together.

Sharanagati's annual three-day spring planting festival draws all of us together, along with neighbors from surrounding valleys and friends from Victoria and Vancouver, Calgary and Kelowna. We plant acres of organic crops: sunchokes, potatoes, carrots, beets, lettuce, tomatoes, greens, cabbage, broccoli, squash, herbs and more. Each afternoon we break for incredibly variegated, energizing, delicious vegetarian feasts,

and at dusk we sing around a bonfire and sometimes have a talent show with skits and musicals. Fall brings a harvest festival with many of the same activities. From ages four to seventy-four, everyone gets involved in the sweet magic of working with the earth and with each other.

To enter the delightful vista of bhakti I'm dependent on my spiritual teacher and the affectionate company of my betters. Through their honest desire to share the valuables they've found, I get hints of how the devotional plant of bhakti will renovate my spirit and choke the weeds of lust, greed, envy, anger, and the desire to control others for my own ends.

I perpetually stand under materially unmotivated servants of God, awaiting their kindness to release me from the grasp of my lower nature and to show me, a *jivatma*, how I can flourish and be all that I am. Other than these rare souls I have no shelter and no hope. One summer, fifty young, enthusiastic spiritualists came to visit us in Sharanagati, and in the evening all of them and we residents sat on the lakeside dock. One of our guests played a harmonium, two played drums, a few others hand cymbals. The sky was pale and cloudless, the air clear, the lake still, and when the mountains resounded to our chorus, the soulful melodies seemed to return with even more freshness and joy than we had put into them – vibrations that rolled back to us as if from innumerable singers hidden in distant forests. Night closed in and life swelled with laughter and gratitude for the incredible privilege of serving God simply by hearing and chanting His names together.

*The propagandist does not desire that his pupils should survey the world and freely choose a purpose which to them appears of value. He desires, like a topiarian artist, that their growth shall be trained and twisted to suit the gardener's purpose. And in thwarting their natural growth he is apt to destroy in them all generous vigor, replacing it by envy, destructiveness, and cruelty.*

— Bertrand Russell

**Of secret things I am silence, and of those who seek victory I am morality. 10.38**

## Silence and Morality

For two miles I've been trudging through eighteen-inch-deep snow; I'm tired and darkness is settling in. If I stop now I will freeze in the night right here, half a mile from home. And what if I did die here? I'm not ready. My daughter's still young, my husband's not a single sort of person, my dreams and schemes lie incomplete. The best of my life is ahead, maybe, if I can overcome my reticent nature. I must keep caring, keep trudging. Step by laborious step I go on, and would get lost were it not for the beacon of my neighbor's bedroom light. At this moment Sharanagati's silence is oppressive: no birds' songs, no breeze stirring the firs, no children's chatter, no life. John is working late in his studio, and Priya has come to our house with her friends and, finding it dark and cold, left with them for the night, not knowing where I am. And where am I? Wistful, alone, yet now confident – ultimately all is well, for I've found the path and will stay on it. Soon I'll be reposed before my own crackling woodstove.

In the winter silence and solitude of Sharanagati I sometimes wonder if I will ever realize basic spiritual truths, if any of my studies and mantra meditations will ever seep beyond the cerebral level and allow me to connect with the spirit. Away from the din and unease of modern life, Sharanagati's silence lets me face the gulf between what I prefer not to be and what I could be. This silence nurtures my desire to be rid of doubt and drawn into deeper understanding; it builds my trust in the secret meaning behind life's mysteries. In this silence my guru's teachings can reach me in their own good time.

I regularly read the headlines in the web edition of the *New York Times* and am jolted by the animosity and posturing that pervades social and

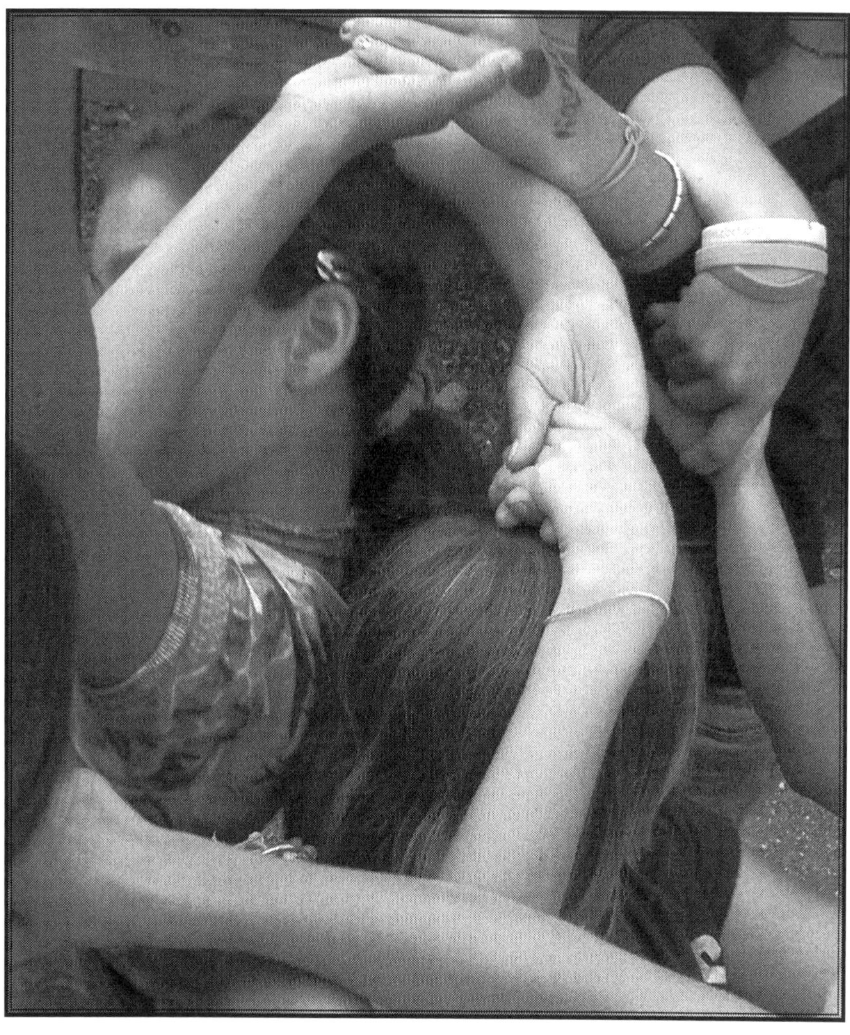

political interactions. People are not dealing well with disagreement, discontent, doubt, despair, restlessness and longing, but are perverting these into violence, depression, intoxication, cheating, rage and frenetic overwork.

> One who is not connected with God can have neither transcendental intelligence nor a steady mind, without which there is no possibility of peace. And how can there be any happiness without peace?
>
> — Bhagavad-gita 2.66

To most, a quiet life of simple toil with minimal worldly ambitions and centered on holiness appears stoic and empty. Yet, if we but silence the mind's racket, the beauty of God-centered simplicity unfolds before us. At any time and in any place we can take the spiritual path toward victory over the mind's clamor. At each moment we can chose how to act and react.

"Of those who seek victory," Krishna says, "I am morality." Not surprisingly, the requisite for spiritual victory is morality.

> In order to approach the purest of the pure, one must become completely pure, and to this end morality and ethics are necessary. Therefore, in our Krishna consciousness movement we prohibit illicit sex, meat-eating, intoxication and gambling – the four pillars of sinful life. If we can avoid these sinful activities, we can remain on the platform of purity. Krishna consciousness is based on this morality, and one who cannot follow these principles falls down from the spiritual platform. Thus, purity is the basic principle of God consciousness and is essential for the re-establishment of our eternal relationship with God.
>
> — Bhaktivedanta Swami Prabhupada

Immorality subverts our inner cry for happiness and harmony with harshness and mental and emotional tumult. It is our degradation and defeat. It's in morality that I find silent, secret strength and I am largely free of the disappointment of not living up to my own expectations. Morality shrinks the separation between God and me.

*The only guide to a man is his conscience; the only shield to his memory is the rectitude and sincerity of his actions ... but with this shield, however the fates may play, we march always in the ranks of honor.*

— Winston Churchill

*In the midst of the hurricane of the material world everything changes very quickly, but if one remains silent and simply observes the actions and reactions of the hurricane, he is understood to be liberated. He remains Krishna conscious, jubilant, despite the material energy.*

— Bhaktivedanta Swami Prabhupada

*The fruit of silence is prayer, the fruit of prayer is faith, the fruit of faith is love, the fruit of love is service.*

— Mother Teresa

**O Krishna, the world becomes joyful upon hearing Your name, and thus everyone becomes attached to You. 11.36**

(Arjuna speaking)

## Prayer

After two days of heavy rain, this morning the clouds cleared to reveal the season's first snow on a nearby ridge. On my walk, the dark, spongy duff softened my footsteps as I watched more than sixty geese, so distant that their honks sounded like cricket chirps, make great circles overhead and finally set off south, forming a vague "v" that seemed like a half-mile strand of floating dust.

Winter approaches and geese go southward, just as life's hardships and uncertainties naturally evoke our prayers. Thus, as they have throughout history, people throughout the world pray. Since the mid-1980s Sharanagati has been a home of prayer, and each time I enter this valley the soft, upraising currents of decades of prayer curl around and cheer me.

Prayer is practically instinctive, but what should I pray for? To pray for good health and success in my endeavors, a happy family and financial ease is to pray for goals as fleeting as the warm days of summer.

> There is no stronger obstruction to one's self-interest than thinking other subject matters to be more pleasing than one's self-realization.
>
> — Srimad-Bhagavatam 4.22.32

Asking God for something transient is like a pauper asking an emperor for a farthing. Why not ask for something lasting – something worthy of who I am?

My prayers reflect my desires and, as much as I understand that I'm a *jivatma* who's temporarily residing in a body composed of matter, I can leave mundane aspirations aside and simply pray, "God, please engage me in Your service." I can pray to act with devotion to God; I can pray

for bhakti. Transcending my body, mind and intelligence, this prayer offers me access to an intangible focal point of grace. It's passage into that mysterious sphere where I, my family and my community can live in happiness and harmony.

To sincerely and purely pray is natural; it's my causeless resistance to prayer that's foreign. My distracted and dry prayers are those of a weary, shortsighted goose who has lost its bearings and is struggling to regain them. But anyway I pray daily: in the dark of the early morning when I first awake, during my long walks through lonely forests, with my husband and daughter in the sacred space in our quaint home, in our local temple, in the homes of friends. I pray to engage in God's service and I pray that I will slough off my lethargy and dullness enough to chant God's names, which are the life of transcendental knowledge, with feeling.

> You have invested all Your potencies in Your holy names, and there are no hard and fast rules for chanting them. Out of kindness You enable us to easily approach You by chanting Your holy names, but I am so unfortunate that I have no attraction for them.
>
> — Chaitanya Charitamrita 3.20.16, Sri Chaitanya speaking

God's transcendental names are not ordinary words but, whether spoken softly – called *japa* – or sung joyfully in chorus – kirtan – are a prayer that has the power to uplift and transform the heart. Even an inattentive person like me feels peaceful and properly situated while praying alone or with prayerful singers. During both *japa* and kirtan I find my thoughts inconsequential, let them go and, simply by hearing the words of the prayerful chanting, experience waves of anomalies: I'm enthusiastic yet patient, confident despite obstacles, hopeful although seriously lacking qualification. Something inside me that wants to take flight becomes a little less fettered.

Removed from the clocks and calendars of ordinary life, in private or in public, prayerful chanting isn't a performance but is a meditation in which everyone who participates is bathed by sacred sound. Chanting God's names strengthens my relationship with God; He, in the form of His name, becomes my ongoing guide and companion.

*In prayer, the principal thing is to stand before God with the mind in the heart, and to go on standing before him unceasingly day and night until the end of life.*

— Bishop Theophan (19th century)

*We are all situated in relative positions according to our own karma. Yet every one of us can offer prayers with heart and soul as far as we can appreciate God's glories. That is our perfection.*

— Bhaktivedanta Swami Prabhupada

*One must learn to call upon the name of God, more even than breathing – at all times, in all places, in every kind of occupation.*

— St. Peter the Damascene

**As a father tolerates the impudence of his son, a friend the impertinence of a friend, or a husband the familiarity of his wife, please tolerate the wrongs I may have done You. 11.44**

(Arjuna speaking)

## Good Will

At our September annual general meeting, we Sharanagati residents elected eleven directors who would make community decisions for the coming year. Under their leadership the year promises to be memorable as these new directors, although quite varied in their opinions and personalities, have much good in common. All of them can listen and learn, can easily relate to those who differ from them, can express their ideas constructively, want to help Sharanagati and its residents prosper, and have mutual good will.

The basis of good will is love. Out of his love for Krishna, Arjuna asks to be forgiven for his transgressions, and out of His munificent love for Arjuna, Krishna readily forgives him.

> As all surrender unto Me, I reward them accordingly. Everyone follows My path in all respects, O Arjuna.
>
> — Bhagavad-gita 4.11, Krishna speaking

What I give to my relationship with God determines how He reciprocates with me. And the same normally holds true in my relationships with others: I get back what I give out. Generally, when I express my concern for others, they are also concerned about me; when I'm attentive to others they reciprocate similarly. These exchanges are due to love, and what is love but to want what's best – to have good will – for the other?

Good will – the desire that each person benefits physically, mentally, emotionally and spiritually – also extends to negative relationships. Toward someone who exploits or abuses others, good will includes anger expressed without grudge or bias, and punishment meted out to rectify. Good will can also mean I disassociate from another; it can mean calling the police, as John and I did when our nineteen-year-old neighbor broke into our house; it can mean graciously accepting unpleasant, unlikely-to-change aspects of a person. Good will isn't stereotyped. It encompasses sternness and softness, gravity and lightheartedness, chastisement and compassion. Because it's based on love and girded by spiritual knowledge and detachment, good will withstands the onslaught of my fluctuating moods, phases and vulnerabilities.

In a world full of "self-help" and "self-improvement" I can easily become self-engrossed and squelch my innate inclination to extend myself for another's good. My own ill will surfaced when a Sharanagati neighbor repeatedly offered visitors a distorted version of spiritual life. I railed and complained to John, held her in the lowest esteem, directed mean thoughts toward her and set her straight through imagined conversations (throughout which she would smile broadly, as she always does).

"I have a problem with the way you speak with Sharanagati guests."

"What's the problem?"

"Well, you just encourage them to do what you're doing."

"That's true, but why shouldn't I? Naturally I share what works for me."

"But there's a bigger picture that guests should know about."

"Hey, I talk to people according to my understanding. I'm not telling you what to say to people, and you don't need to tell me."

"But I do need to tell you. That's why I'm doing it." But she sauntered off, still smiling.

I finally noticed that these mental exchanges didn't help my neighbor or me.

Ill will is my responsibility alone. I cannot command it to change, but I can control how I act and what I say. Even if I don't feel like it, I can choose to act and speak as if I had good will. This isn't artificial or forced, but a reflection of who I really am – a *jivatma*, an integral part of God, who has only good will for all beings. It's ill will that's artificial. I don't have to act according to ill will's dictates but, even when my emotions disagree, can act with good will. By tolerating whatever happens and by depending on my innate good will, which comes from the good will of God, a new dimension unfolds.

> Dear God, those who earnestly wait for You to bestow Your causeless mercy upon them, all the while patiently suffering the reactions of their past misdeeds and offering You respectful obeisances with their heart, words and body, are surely eligible for liberation, for it has become their rightful claim.
>
> — Srimad-Bhagavatam 10.14.8

To receive my parents' inheritance I simply had to remain alive, and similarly by the good will of God I'll feel good will toward other people – even troublesome ones – if I but remain spiritually alive. With the dignity worthy of a spiritual being, in good will I do not blame or complain or accuse others, but remember my goal – to serve God with love – and relate to others on the basis of achieving it. I don't allow pride to strangle my good will and narrow my vision so that "winning" a dispute seems like a victory. When I "win," what's often lost is good will. Once I sat in on mediation between two Sharanagati residents and witnessed the power of letting each person speak his mind while the other paid full attention, the value of considered questions, the magic of respectful responses. At the end, these two men weren't close friends, but they understood each other and found a course of action that satisfied them both.

Good will helps resolve relationship problems; with freshness and vigor it enables each person to try to understand the other's feelings and to find fair solutions based on merit and mutual gain. And good will allows me to be happy even if I don't solve all my problems or overcome all adversity.

With good will I respect others' personalities and am therefore gentle and polite and let others be perfectly themselves. My husband and I encourage our daughter to find and pursue her calling. So far, she loves

playing the flute, singing, sports and everything to do with horses. Some of John's and my interests are quite different, but those enthuse her.

Good will reveals subtle textures and tints in formerly stilted and sterile ways of thinking. Good will discovers unity within differences. Good will renews my creative power and reminds me of my own value and the heights to which I am meant to strive. With my neighbor who offers distorted spirituality, I foresaw no benefit from mediation so I meditated on how she was acting according to her understanding, and how my distress was from imposing my understanding on her. It didn't cure the problem, but let me relax about it. I extend good will to her by avoiding an argument that will only separate us more, and on a social level we're friendly. In good will I do not proselytize or take narcissistic satisfaction in my own ways.

Good will is vulnerable to pain and yet continues. It lessens the expectations I have of others, enlarges what I expect from myself and nurtures affinity. It lets me appreciate my companions' qualities and know the satisfaction of using myself well to benefit another.

Ill will criticizes the fault within the person; good will speaks to the person behind the fault. Good will, the potency of the *jivatma*, allows me to laugh at my whimsical mind and its foibles. Besides humor, a remarkable sense of detachment and equality accompanies good will, for it shrinks my own conceit and makes me aware that I am simply a friend among friends. I move closer to the importance, the uniqueness and the sameness of all life.

Good will, a result of recognizing the spiritual identity of each individual, creates realizations as multifaceted as the *jivatma* is beautiful. Through God's unparalleled ingenuity, good will solves the insoluble.

Good will is also free will: it's when we decide to manifest acceptance, compassion, forgiveness and cooperation. It radiates from us – the *jivatma* – and wants to expand to encompass each *jivatma* we contact. Good will, God's gift to the grateful *jivatma*, is a victory over illusion. How to best show it is not always easy or clear but is always necessary, for good will initiates an ecstatic dance of freedom that, in spite of everything, creates harmony.

*If anyone says, 'I love God' and hates his brother, he is a liar: for he who does not love his brother whom he has seen cannot love God whom he has not seen.*

— I John 4.20

*May there be good fortune throughout the universe, and may all envious persons be pacified. May all living entities become calm by practicing bhakti-yoga, for by accepting devotional service they will think of each other's welfare. Therefore let us all engage in the service of the supreme transcendence, Krishna, and always remain absorbed in thought of Him.*

— Srimad-Bhagavatam 5.18.9

*Your neighbors are the channel through which all your virtues come to birth.*
— St. Catherine of Siena

**One who works for Me, who makes Me the supreme goal of life, and who is friendly to every living being – that person certainly comes to Me.**
**11.55**

## Friendship

As mutual trust grows, friendship blossoms.

A Sharanagati opulence is a core group of residents who have served God together since the 1970s, and from these decades of bhakti – devotional service – are united in friendship.

Also since the early '70s, Yamuna Devi, Donna and I have been friends and have shared confidences and laughter, confusion and grief, and an abiding love for our guru. Yamuna is an internationally renowned and award-winning cook and cookbook author, and for the pleasure of guru and God some of our service together has centered on cooking – I've cooked under Yamuna's tutelage, tested her recipes and photographed her exquisite dishes.

Yamuna and Donna are our closest neighbors, and entering their Sharanagati home, a straw bale house they built with the help of two resident builders, I am enveloped by a kindly ambience. I first notice the far wall covered with books on tipsy homemade wood bookshelves that look like they may one day crash but never do. Elegant, classic paintings of Krishna with His friends and cows hang on the walls. In the windows are traditional stained glass designs, handmade by Yamuna, each colored to match the decor. I take off my jacket and hang it on one of the thick home-carved hooks over the wood bin in the mud room. On going into the main room, I'm gratified to see that the flowers – both the silk ones and the exotic garden lilies – that I've given to Donna and Yamuna are decorating their altar. Welcomed with heartfelt sincerity by the two of them, I feel perfectly situated and loved. These devoted

women befriend all who come to their home, and make even a common neighbor like me feel special; around them my feeble impetus to please God and His devotees gains momentum. To enter their home is to enter the culture of consideration.

One winter when I had to leave Sharanagati for some time, these friends regularly sent John and Priya hot thick homemade soups and biscuits, and when I heard about their care my heart was warmed as much as my family was nourished. Without these neighbors' love, my life would be incomplete.

Devotional friends graciously and effortlessly overlook race, gender, nationality, religion, deficiencies, handicaps and IQ to see you, a *jivatma*, a unique spiritual being. With these friends you can relax and be yourself, for they accept you the way you are. When you're in difficulty, they magnify your strengths, minimize your weaknesses, and enable you to accept your situation and to see the lesson and its blessing. When I broke my arm in a bicycle accident, my neighbors offered me solace and reminded me that nothing is an accident and that this injury too would pass. I surrendered to being an invalid and settled into a healing lifestyle.

At some point in our spiritual evolution, when our friendships extend past former artificial boundaries, to our joy we'll have more friends.

> We are all simply living entities playing on a stage in the dress of father, mother, children, friend, enemy, sinner and saint, etc. It is like a great drama with so many characters playing their parts. However, on the stage a person may be an enemy or whatever, but off the stage all the actors are friends. Similarly, with these bodies we are playing on the stage of material nature, and we attach so many designations to one another ... all the multifarious relationships between bodies are just so much stage play. One who is actually realized and has actually attained yoga no longer sees these bodily distinctions.
>
> — Bhaktivedanta Swami Prabhupada

Through their love, true friends express their own spiritual identity, *jivatma*. Their friendship is not passive; they respond generously to the many demands in their lives. Enlarging their circle to include more friends, they find glory in the extraordinary similarities and differences of these new friends and are eager to hear and benefit from their views. When conflict arises friends maintain respect and trust, feeling like allies rather than adversaries. Instead of clinging tightly to their own sound opinion, for the love of God and one another, they may let it go.

Once, Yamuna, Donna and I differed over whether a certain family should take up residence in Sharanagati. We heard each other out and, realizing that both sides of the argument had merit, finally agreed with the majority of Sharanagati-ites and welcomed the new family to the community. To refuse to find common ground with another when reason or occasion demand it is a sign of pride and stubbornness. A friend who does so or who alienates is inattentive, ungrateful; one who seeks his or her own prominence is only the shadow of a friend.

Spiritual friendship is grounded in integrity. Its spaciousness is warmed by affection, lit with cheerfulness and vivified by bhakti. Over all are God's intimate, protective blessings. Where individuals, families and communities share devotional friendship, spiritual health and happiness are nurtured day by day.

*All of you are engaged in one occupation – devotional service. I am so pleased with your mutual friendship that I wish you all good fortune.*

— Srimad-Bhagavatam 4.30.8, Krishna speaking

*The most exhausting thing in life, I have discovered, is being insincere. That is why so much of social life is exhausting; one is wearing a mask. I have shed my mask.*

— Ann Morrow Lindbergh

*If you treat a person as he is, he will stay as he is; but if you treat him as if he were what he ought to be and could be, he will become what he ought to be and could be.*

— Johann Wolfgang von Goethe

*Love is not love which alters when it alteration finds.*

— William Shakespeare

*Even*
*After*
*All this time*
*The sun never says to the earth,*
*"You owe*
*Me."*
*Look*
*What happens*
*With a love like that,*
*It lights the*
*Whole*
*Sky.*

— Hafez

**That person by whom no one is put into difficulty and who is not disturbed by anyone, who is equipoised in happiness and distress, fear and anxiety, is very dear to Me. 12.15**

## All-Inclusive Worthiness

Habitually I align myself with those I consider "worthy" and distance myself from those who, for whatever reason, I consider "unworthy." But in God's vision everyone is worthy. He asks that I cast aside my superiority complex and see others as He sees them.

When a dog snaps at me and his smiling owner, a Sharanagati resident, yells over the dog's barks, "He's never bitten anybody yet!" am I supposed to be undisturbed and see that person and her dog as worthy of respect?

One way or another, confrontations abound, and without being intimidated or resentful I must deal with them, accepting the mysterious uniqueness of the persons I encounter. Valuing these persons for the qualities they have, I try to stop seeking in them qualities they lack and try to address the issue at hand along with its underlying emotions. As for the dog, I simply arm myself with a worthy stick.

Due in part to her dog's behavior, I readily dismiss my dog-owner neighbor, effectively nullifying any possibility of neighborliness between us. But if I disdain her I can easily disdain others, and by snobbery bring tension and distance to my relationships.

If, however, I accept everyone as worthy of respect, by God's grace even discord can lead to the revelation that ultimately He is behind diversity. One morning my Sharanagati neighbor decided to introduce me to her dog.

"If you get to know Blacky, he won't treat you the way he does."

"Really? Do you think so?"

"Yeah, he barks at you because he doesn't know you."

"I'm not sure about that. I've been walking by your house regularly for years now, and every time your dog makes a ruckus."

My neighbor took the unwilling Blacky by his collar and pulled him over to me, had him sniff my clothes, told him my name and explained to him that I wasn't a threat. The next time I walked by her house Blacky barked and snapped at me as usual. Yet, there was a difference. For the first time I understood that Blacky's aggression was from his loyalty to his owner, and her defense of him was from gratitude – her husband's a bus driver and much of the time Blacky is her only companion. But this little insight into the background behavioral dynamics didn't prepare me for Blacky's owner's next diagnosis: "He's still barking at you because you're not seeing all beings equally." Astonished, I could only laugh and wonder which was greater, my lack of spiritual vision or her lack of dog training skills.

> In the material world there are varieties, but there is no agreement. In the spiritual world there are varieties, but there is agreement. That is the difference. The materialist, without being able to adjust the varieties and the disagreements, makes everything zero. They cannot come into agreement with varieties; but if we keep Krishna in the center, then there will be agreement in varieties. This is called unity in diversity.
>
> — Bhaktivedanta Swami Prabhupada

Although my relationship with some dogs and their owners is lacking, I rest in the conviction that all living beings are *jivatmas* – spiritual in essence. Bhakti, devotional service, is the *jivatma's* expression of love for God, for other *jivatmas* and for God's creation. Bhakti, the foundation of harmony, inspires faith, self-discipline and humility. Bhakti, however, is not easily attained because to get past the mundane, to see the *jivatma* in the barking dog, is difficult. But even without realizing *jivatma's* presence, I can still sense the worth of all beings.

Bhakti ushers an aliveness that soothes the heart and, flowing past all boundaries, all externals and all failures, inspires me to grow despite my shortcomings and mistakes. It's an excursion out of time that thaws my frozen sincerity. I touch the beauty of God and the eternal worthiness of His every created being. No one is left out. A new, sustainable, underlying happiness rises.

*If we learn how to love Krishna, then it is very easy to immediately and simultaneously love every living being. It is like pouring water on the root of a tree or supplying food to one's stomach.*

— Bhaktivedanta Swami Prabhupada

*One should observe all living entities to be on the same level as oneself. This means that no one should be neglected as inferior; because the Supersoul is seated in everyone's body, everyone should be respected as a temple of God.*

— Chanakya Pandit

**Humility, pridelessness, nonviolence, tolerance, simplicity, approaching a bona fide spiritual master, cleanliness, steadiness and self-control – these I declare to be knowledge, and the lack thereof is ignorance. 13.8**

## Humility

The word "humility" comes from the Latin humus, meaning "earth," "ground," and "lowly." Humus, however, is much more than lowly earth: it's the richest of all earth; it's organic, dark, friable soil that's poised to support life. Seeds thrive in humus, and so from humus the food that sustains earthly life is produced. Such a vital yet neglected substance is appropriately connected to the word humility, for humility alone is the attitude that sustains spiritual life.

> Beginning from practicing humility up to the point of realization of the Supreme Truth, the Absolute Personality of Godhead, this process is just like a staircase beginning from the ground floor and going up to the top floor.
>
> — Bhaktivedanta Swami Prabhupada

Humility makes holiness possible; it's an expression of knowledge, it's the root of trustworthy intelligence, and its by-products are tolerance and a love for all that is genuine.

To awaken our dormant humility is to do something great: to be what we are – small and fallen. If I can admit that I don't know much about transcendence and that I have not progressed much on the transcendental path, I feel comfortable in that frankness. My longing for admiration wanes.

> Our disease is desire for that which is material; even while advancing in spiritual life, we want material acclaim. One must be freed from this disease.
>
> — Bhaktivedanta Swami Prabhupada

Pride, on the other hand, comes with the weighty price tag of stress: "What about me – my pleasure, my position, my prestige?" On this altar of self-importance, ambition and control, I sacrifice my happiness and blockade myself spiritually. Many spiritual leaders have visited Sharanagati over the years, and most of them can accurately present God-conscious philosophy. But our love goes to those of them who are more eager to give than to receive, who focus on us more than on themselves. By their example these leaders teach us humility and inspire our devotion to God.

> Pride is the root of all evil ... pride is the beginning of all sin. Seven principal vices spring doubtless from this poisonous root, namely, vainglory, envy, anger, melancholy, avarice, gluttony and lust.
>
> — St. Gregory the Great

If I choose not to humble myself before what is greater than me I am captured by what is less than me – pride and its mundane effects. Inevitably, I am disappointed and dissatisfied. Pride creates inner violence – it's an attitude that contradicts our essence – for innately the *jivatma* is humble. To be humble is as natural as walking on the ground.

A humble heart extends itself to others and deals modestly with them. It's jubilant, friendly, forgiving and caring. Instead of fantasizing about personal perfection – a self-indulgent and hollow line of thinking – the humble are pleased to voice others' good qualities.

> If I do not like to give honor to others, then my self-seeking is present and can be traced. But when I can give honor without wanting honor for myself, I will be qualified to search for Krishna, the Absolute.
>
> — B. R. Sridhar Swami

The truly humble have abandoned every attempt at being humble and instead have entered into a whole new dimension of existence, where the unimaginable greatness and the incomparable perfection of God overshadows their own smallness and faults. Such persons are less and less subject to their fickle mind and the dictates of society. Grounded in an authentic spiritual tradition, daily spiritual practice and ordinary tasks, the humble respond to people and events with empathy and grace. They are spiritually alive and happy in their own situation. The vulnerability of humility fructifies in this strength and freedom.

Bhagavad-gita informs us how to live fully, as we are meant to live, and how we can share that fullness with others. As a gardener joyfully shares the bounty of the rich soil, so God graciously makes His bounty accessible to the humble. It's the humble who do not harm the earth for they avoid waste and are satisfied without extravagance.

In reciprocation, God provides the most necessary thing of all: the rich inner harvest of genuine meaning and love. Bhaktivedanta Swami Prabhupada explains that humility "is the cause of proportionate spiritual realization, by which one can ultimately meet God in person, as a person meets another person face to face."

*We belong to God. Yet so does everybody else belong to God. We just happen to be conscious of it, and to make a profession out of this consciousness. But does that entitle us to consider ourselves different, or even better than others? The whole idea is preposterous.*

— Thomas Merton

*There is no greater human presumption than to read the mind of the Almighty, and no more dangerous individual than the one who has convinced himself that he is executing the Almighty's will.*

— Arthur Schlesinger, Jr.

**Nature is said to be the cause of all material causes and effects, whereas the living entity is the cause of the various sufferings and enjoyments in this world. 13.21**

## Misery

Arjuna's mental misery impelled him to cry for help. In response, Krishna told Arjuna that he could not avoid the conflict that caused his misery, but he could view his misery differently and do his duty despite it. Krishna's words, Bhagavad-gita, did not change Arjuna's circumstances but his consciousness.

Although they're not always visible, misery and suffering pervade life. Mental, emotional and physical disturbances create misery and suffering, but how we deal with these – the consciousness with which we bear our troubles – is up to us. In all circumstances we have the

power to choose our attitude. Bhagavad-gita doesn't put a Band-Aid on misery but throws open a window of comprehension on it. Through knowledge, Bhagavad-gita empowers us to face misery constructively.

> The living entities are blessed or damned with circumstances according to their past desire and activity. According to one's desires and activities, material nature places one in various residential quarters. The beings themselves are the cause of their attaining such residential quarters and their attendant enjoyment or suffering.
>
> — Bhaktivedanta Swami Prabhupada

When facing any type of suffering I have three choices: to try to change the situation and/ or the person who is apparently causing the suffering; to suffer; to change my attitude.

Since I don't want to suffer it's natural that I will try, within reason, to change whatever it is that caused my suffering. If I find that despite my best efforts I cannot avoid the suffering, I'm left with the other two choices: to suffer or to change my attitude. Those on the spiritual path don't bemoan unavoidable suffering. They accept it with grace. Misery has come unasked for, but I tolerate and adjust – with hope rather than resignation – and focus on bhakti, devotional service. I accept that I'm not in complete control of what happens to me; I acknowledge a will greater than mine that has my best interests at heart.

> In all reverse conditions, devotees agree to suffer the results of their past lives. They never accuse God of putting them into a distressed condition. When suffering reversals, devotees always consider that the reverse conditions are God's concessions. They are never angry with their master; they are always satisfied with the position their master offers.
>
> — Srimad-Bhagavatam 10.14.8

In choosing to accept the inevitable I can rise above my fate. Each moment I can decide not to submit to those forces that would make me forget my identity and calling, that would make me become a toy of time and place, that would make me bitter, angry, resentful and cynical. Remembering who I am – a *jivatma* – is an inner achievement worthy of me.

In the tiny town twenty miles to our north lived a middle-aged man who couldn't stay in the Sharanagati community. When he was two years old he'd fallen down a flight of stairs and been crippled. Ever since, he was often pain-ridden. He told me his story one morning, sitting in his wheelchair in his sunny, spotless apartment. I was struck by his cheerfulness and his devotion – the altar in his living room practically glowed from his loving care. He needed central heating and electricity, wheelchair access and shopping facilities, so he lived in town and helped Sharanagati residents from his apartment – he was computer savvy and solved some technical problems for me. I admired him for keeping what's important – devotional service to God and His devotees – in the forefront of his life. A few years later he passed away, and my neighbors who knew him well eulogized him. More than I had realized, he was a saint, and the bodily miseries he'd tolerated and transcended increased his glories.

I've seen a mother's love for her infant obliterate the suffering she experienced during childbirth and during her serious postpartum complications. Similarly our love for God and guru can obliterate our suffering, turning it into a small, inevitable component in the process of getting the company of the persons we love and who love us. Love's incredible potency transforms suffering into something we not only bear with dignity, but even overlook.

Sharanagati's waving land, its smiling sky, its curved grass that pokes up from beneath layers of snow, its expanse of white-peaked mountains lit with glaring sunlight all somehow support Bhagavad-gita's teachings of transcending misery. In the rapturous song of the yellow-throated warbler, in the distant hum of frogs against the vast silence, in the silent march of the clouds, there's symmetry and cycles. As the days pass and I observe creation, development, dwindling and death, I see misery, glory and beauty in each phase. It leads me sometimes to wonder what my own physical dwindling will be like, how I will handle it and how it will affect my next birth. I wonder if I'll ever be ready for death and what that will be like, who will be there for me and if, before that, I can be there for others. Warmly dressed I stomp through the snow, leaving tracks, following tracks, my eyes watery from the invigorating sting of cold on my face.

Bhagavad-gita puts misery in a kaleidoscope and transforms it from bits of random bad luck to a thought-provoking pattern. For misery, Bhagavad-gita prescribes the balm of detachment, the tender touch of fortitude, the sweet inner joy of wisdom, and most of all, bhakti.

*Love, thy power and spell benign*
*Now melt this soul to God*
*How can these earthly words describe*
*This feeling so soft and broad.*

— Bhaktivinode Thakur

*Because matter is destructible, through the material condition the* jivatma *suffers. Otherwise, the* jivatma *is detached from all material conditions.*

— Bhaktivedanta Swami Prabhupada

*The biggest troublemaker you'll probably ever have to deal with watches you shave his face in the mirror every mornin'.*

— Old farmer's adage

**Material nature consists of three modes – goodness, passion and ignorance. When the eternal living entity comes in contact with nature, O mighty-armed Arjuna, it becomes conditioned by these modes. 14.5**

## Material Nature

The qualities of goodness, passion and ignorance constrain the *jivatmas* in this world. Influenced by goodness, a person is dispassionate and attracted to knowledge for its own sake. In passion one hankers for and makes strenuous efforts to obtain objects of desire. And a person influenced by ignorance is lazy, apathetic and oblivious. In other words, consciousness conditioned by goodness is alert and attentive yet detached; consciousness conditioned by passion is excited and focuses narrowly on desired objects; and consciousness conditioned by ignorance is unaware, uncaring and distracted.

Like most people, I'm alternately influenced by various combinations of these qualities. Sometimes I'm jolly and content (goodness), while at other times I'm dissatisfied, restless and anxious (passion). And from time to time I'm bewildered (ignorance). Although I think I'm in control, in fact, I'm controlled by these qualities like a hapless rider on a runaway horse.

> The bewildered spirit soul thinks itself the doer of activities that are in actuality carried out by the three modes of material nature.
>
> — Bhagavad-gita 3.27

> Everyone is like a play toy in the hands of the illusory energy and is acting as it moves him.
>
> — Bhaktivedanta Swami Prabhupada

When I peek at the stark reality of my situation I want to free myself from these powerful forces. But on my own, I – small, weak and uncertain – cannot succeed. In Sharanagati I gain strength – from the wildness of it and from the absence of meaningless social demands and society's numbing culture of consumption. Here friendships fortify me and I'm challenged to use my time well. And here I observe goodness, passion and ignorance pushing me and others around. We go from grouchy to gracious, from foolish to frustrated, from carefree to duty-bound, from passionately active to annoyingly inactive, from cooperative to reclusive. Like everywhere else, this valley has the benefits and burdens of every mood and personality type. Although we residents have common ideals and goals, we jostle together and misunderstand, disagree and get upset with each other. We complain about the messy people among us, we're disappointed with the irresponsible, we tire of the zealous and overtalkative, we avoid the sentimental and selfish – and at some point we ourselves are each of these.

But as I understand material nature's modes, the influences of passion and ignorance wane. I see that in ignorance I hurt others by not caring about them and by being thoughtless, and in passion I have an obnoxious me-first mentality. Only in goodness do I become the generous yet balanced person I want to be: the one who gives often yet who also sees to her own needs on issues of importance. In goodness I'm pleased to care for others – and I care for myself without selfishness and undue expectations of others.

Beyond the mode of goodness, however, there is another stage.

> One is always a servant of lusty desires, anger, greed, illusion, envy and so forth, but if one obtains sufficient strength in spiritual advancement, one can control them. One who obtains such control will always be transcendentally situated, untouched by the modes of material nature. This is only possible when one fully engages in the service of God as God Himself says, "One

> who engages in unalloyed devotional service to Me [bhakti] transcends the modes of material nature and is immediately elevated to the spiritual platform."
>
> — Bhaktivedanta Swami Prabhupada

Rather than be helplessly controlled by the forces of material nature, I can do some service – even a small service – in God consciousness. To serve God with devotion – bhakti – is to serve someone beyond the control of goodness, passion and ignorance. My unique offering of service with word, thought or deed fulfills and uplifts me. There is nothing more beautiful or meaningful, nothing that can help me more than bhakti – the *jivatmas'* everlasting expression of love for God and for one another. The seed of bhakti, implanted by the guru in the sincere heart and nourished by hearing and speaking about God, grows to transport me beyond the influence of goodness, passion and ignorance. I blossom.

To try for bhakti and to share its spiritually nurturing qualities far surpasses the goals of prosperity, prestige and power, for such worldly goals are a landscape of mirages. Bhaktivedanta Swami Prabhupada writes, "Krishna will give you intelligence how to engage in honest, brilliant, glorious work on His behalf [bhakti]." In the activities of my Sharanagati neighbors, whether building a stone addition to their home to accommodate their teenage daughters, or making a garden archway from graceful forest wood, or creating a multicourse feast for guests, the intent is to please guru and God.

With bhakti we will be innocently confident, with childlike faith in God, and undeterred by difficulty. We will feel 'giving' and spontaneous yet determined and courageous, powerful yet peaceful, enthusiastic yet patient. Engaging in bhakti is the most sublime and natural way to live. Anything else is fleeting, insignificant and neglects our best interests. Bhakti is meant to be integral to our life at all times.

> Whatever you do, whatever you eat, whatever you offer or give away, and whatever austerities you perform – do that as an offering to Me.
>
> — Bhagavad-gita 9.27, Krishna speaking

When I feel myself swayed by ignorance and passion I immerse myself in Bhagavad-gita and meditate on how bhakti is unassuming – an act done with bhakti may look like an ordinary act – yet is the embodiment of power, for it attracts God Himself. Although He has everything, our love for God miraculously draws Him to us.

Bhakti is a source of joy, of warmth, of hope, of irrepressible success. Its energy and the attitude it creates benefits me and others, clearing our paths and relieving our minds. Even small acts done with bhakti can mean more than we can imagine. When the crippled Sharanagati supporter who lived in the nearby town passed away one evening in early May, the nurses who attended him remarked on his peaceful and cheerful mood. Others they'd seen in a condition similar to his were bitter, afraid and self-pitying. Our friend, however, was glad to leave his pain-riddled body and felt God's protection. God never fails to reciprocate His servant's love, and our friend's composure and focus was God's grace.

Bhakti inspires me to be all I was meant to be. Freeing me of biases and agendas, bhakti offers me a fresh appreciation for the sacred in ordinary life. And what is sacred? Whatever can be used in God's service. By my nature I must serve – we are all servants – and I can use what I have to please guru and God. I can make an altar for God and beautify it with flowers; I can make my home an ashram, a place where my family and I hear and speak about God. The sovereignty of bhakti transforms the ordinary to the extraordinary. Words become a song, steps become a dance, and our constant companion becomes God Himself.

Bhakti, devotional service to God, a realm of divine attractiveness, nurtures my rapport with every person in my life.

*Somehow the world is hungry for goodness, recognizes it when it sees it, and has an incredible response to the good. There's something in all of us that hungers after the good and true, and when we glimpse it in people we applaud them for it. We long to be just a little like them.*

— Archbishop Desmond Tutu

*The contamination in the heart of a conditioned soul is like a huge accumulation of garbage created by the three modes of material nature, especially the modes of passion and ignorance. This contamination becomes manifest in the form of lusty desires and greed for material possessions.*

— Bhaktivedanta Swami Prabhupada

*As soon as irrevocable loving service – bhakti – is established in the heart, the effects of nature's modes of passion and ignorance, such as lust, desire and hankering, disappear from the heart. Then one becomes completely happy.*

— Srimad-Bhagavatam 1.2.19

*The bhakti tradition found a full expression in the ancient Bhagavad-gita, "The Song of the Lord."*

— Dr. Diane Eck

4

# The Wellspring of Harmony

*Krishna has described* jivatma, *material nature, time and activity to Arjuna. He will now also explain Himself. Some readers will take Krishna's words as allegorical or mythological, but by taking them as fact, then the astonishing vision of reality Krishna gives Arjuna is also a simple, beautiful fact. Although this vision is more than we can experience with unaided eyes, we were made to see it – and to be carried by it from the darkness of confusion to the clearing where deception cannot affect us.*

> When your intelligence has passed out of the dense forest of delusion, you shall become indifferent to all that has been heard and all that is to be heard.
>
> — Bhagavad-gita 2.52

*With eyes clear of prejudice, selfish ends, and mundane attitudes, we will see the supernatural where it is: everywhere. And we will see that the supernatural is ultimately a person. Devotion to Him charms the heart and attracts the mind. To evoke spiritual consciousness is a great and lasting achievement that leads to genuine happiness and harmony.*

**I am the basis of the impersonal Brahman, which is immortal, imperishable and eternal and is the constitutional position of ultimate happiness. 14.27**

## Brahman, the Effulgence

When we first moved in, our house was a fixer-upper; among many other things, the woodstove was broken and needed to be replaced. We looked at used stoves, inexpensive new stoves, and free stoves and finally bought the best woodstove available. Completely airtight, it has a "double burn" feature that creates heat from particles in the smoke, and a system of vents and baffles that makes it the epitome of efficiency. As consciousness originates from the *jivatma* and spreads throughout the body, warmth radiates throughout our home from that stove.

This analogy can extend to include everything:

> As a fire, although existing in one place, can expand its light and heat everywhere, so God, although situated in His spiritual abode, expands Himself everywhere, in both the material and spiritual worlds, by His various energies.
>
> — Vishnu Purana 1.22.52

Just as our individual consciousness – the *jivatma's* energy – spreads all over our body and we feel it in every hair follicle, just as heat, fire's energy, spreads from our woodstove to every square inch of our house, so God, although in one place, has energy present everywhere.

> Everything is but a transformation of the energy of God.
>
> — Chaitanya Charitamrita 1.7.121

This energy of God is called Brahman and is ever subordinate to Him. God is the basis of Brahman, which is the eternal source and resting place of everything, which has no beginning and which lies beyond the cause and effect of this material world. Brahman is God's shining rays, His impersonal, all-pervasive aspect.

The scriptures describe Brahman as inconceivable to material senses, without qualities, formless and incomprehensible. As from one truth, other truths are created – from wood comes fire, heat and light – so everything is a transformation of Brahman, God's energy. And although God's energy transforms from one thing to another, He Himself does not change. He remains the same. Just as, for countless generations, the sun has sent its warm brilliant rays into our valley but itself has remained the same, and as our stove will convert wood into heat but remain the same, so by His energy – Brahman – God does everything in the material and spiritual worlds yet He Himself is never affected by these actions and reactions. God's all-pervading energy, Brahman, transforms into everything we know and eternally comes from the eternal Person, God.

*Although God transforms His innumerable energies, He remains unchanged.*

— Chaitanya Charitamrita 1.7.125

*In a sense, there is nothing but God. Yet nothing is God save and except His transcendental personality. Nothing is different from God but God is different from everything.*

— William H. Deadwyler, III, PhD

*Everything rests upon God, and everything is but an expansion of His energies, but this does not mean that everything is as worshipable as God Himself. The material expansion is temporary, but God is not temporary. The living entities are parts of God, but they are not God Himself.*

— Bhaktivedanta Swami Prabhupada

*For those whose minds are attached to the unmanifested, impersonal feature of God, advancement is very troublesome. To make progress in that discipline is always difficult for those who are embodied.*

— Bhagavad-gita 12.5

*O my Lord, sustainer of all that lives, Your real face is covered by Your dazzling effulgence. Please remove that covering and exhibit Yourself to Your pure devotee.*

— Sri Isopanisad Mantra 15

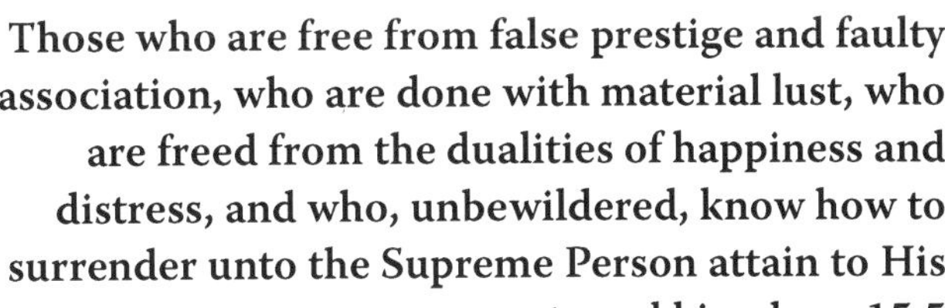

**Those who are free from false prestige and faulty association, who are done with material lust, who are freed from the dualities of happiness and distress, and who, unbewildered, know how to surrender unto the Supreme Person attain to His eternal kingdom. 15.5**

## Obstacles

My daily attempt to advance spiritually is integral to my life, and that attempt is fraught with obstacles. False prestige – the notion that self-importance leads to fulfillment – is one such obstacle. Succumbing to this notion, I'm caught up in posturing and become hollow, alienated from myself.

Another obstacle, faulty association – the scientists, philosophers and others who have eliminated God from their concept of possibility – leads me back to atheism.

> Acting from within the cores of the hearts of all philosophers, who propagate various views, God causes them to forget their own souls while sometimes agreeing and sometimes disagreeing among themselves.
>
> — Srimad-Bhagavatam 6.4.31

> Such philosophers say that this world is unreal, with no foundation, no God in control. They say it is produced of sex desire and has no cause other than lust.
>
> — Bhagavad-gita 16.8

> Because He is all-powerful, God is not subject to the conditioned soul's arguments regarding His existence or nonexistence.
>
> — Bhaktivedanta Swami Prabhupada

God's will directs all things, orders and governs all agents, moves movers and causes causes, drives drivers and rules rulers. Even those who theorize about His nonexistence are unknowingly under His will. Such atheists make poor company, but at their last breath will have God's company, for He says, "I am all-devouring death" (Bhagavad-gita 10.34).

Lust (kama), yet another obstacle, is huge.

> Lusty desires are very strong in everyone, and they are the greatest impediment to the discharge of devotional service.
>
> — Bhaktivedanta Swami Prabhupada

Impelled by my senses and mind I'm a slave of unhealthy eating habits, lust, anger, envy and avarice. But I don't have to yield to these urges. I can resist their force by learning to detach myself from and observe them as I detachedly observe a snowstorm from my favorite couch. Like the storm, lusts' attacks pass – they go as they came – and simply knowing this fact and using my time and energy productively – with an awareness of God – I can find self-control. Otherwise, without self-control, sensual urges can snow me under. Bhagavad-gita warns and prompts me, "Lust, sheltered in your mind and senses, is dragging you, bound and gagged, into the drifts of future misery. This rogue is kidnapping you."

When two foundational pillars gird my intelligence – that my worldly existence is fleeting and that my identity is spiritual – I'll realize that my battle with lust is so significant that I cannot risk losing it and returning to the darkness from which I've been gradually emerging. Even if I flounder in battle, my sense of material momentariness and spiritual momentousness can grant me respite from lust's degrading commands.

Yet another obstacle is the web of dualities – happiness and distress, pleasure and pain, honor and dishonor, good and bad – that holds me securely. Of course, happiness, pleasure, honor and good seem desirable, but "duality" means that the other half – the undesirable half – will inescapably come in due time, just as summer follows winter. Duality exhausts and foils me.

> The nonpermanent appearance of happiness and distress, and their disappearance in due course, are like the appearance and disappearance of winter and summer seasons. They arise from sense perception, and one must learn to tolerate them without being disturbed.
>
> — Bhagavad-gita 2.14

To feverishly seek happiness by catering to my likes and running from my dislikes increases my false hopes while diminishing my actual pleasure. Happiness comes not by seeking it, but by absorbing myself in what is greater than I am, and I find it in my feelings of insignificance before the firmament, in witnessing the unstoppable flow of the changing seasons, in the spirit behind my friends' camaraderie, in my divine service. And distress diminishes by gradual spiritual maturation. Before my husband and I moved to Sharanagati, every couple of years we'd move from one city to another, always thinking that the next place would be right for us. When we got to this glen we finally noticed that we'd been carrying inside ourselves everything we needed to be happy.

To tolerate dualities dismantles a barrier between me and God.

Finally, overcoming all obstacles, God wants me to come to Him.

Beyond time and material nature, mindfulness and morality, ethics and duality, concepts and cynicism, there's a Person who controls it all. That eternal Supreme Person, God, is the wellspring of all that exists. He has a name and a form, as well as qualities and activities. A proper analysis of this world – His energy – will finally bring me, lost in wonder and humbled at my privilege, to Him, the Supreme Source of all, including the effulgent Brahman. Yet, as I did in former years, many shy away, uneasy and upset by this conclusion.

Engrossed in the silence and loveliness of a deep forest, it's astounding to realize there is an intimate yet inconceivable Person with me. I am stilled and awed.

He is with me. Acknowledging Him, I make my daily struggles into a beautiful life. Adversity and loss surround me, but so does the divine presence behind my daily tasks and difficulties. My security rests in the strength of my connection with Him. By asking basic and relevant questions of any proposed course of action – Is it righteous? Is it wise? Is it pleasing to God and His devotees? – and responding appropriately, obstacles that were once boulders pulverize into pebbles.

*The conditioned soul is always attracted by the external energy. Therefore he is subjected to lust and greed, and he suffers under the conditions of material nature.*

— Bhaktivedanta Swami Prabhupada

*Argument, false prestige and lack of discrimination are the roots of entanglement in the material world.*

— Srimad-Bhagavatam 5.13.22

**That supreme abode of Mine is not illumined by the sun or moon, nor by fire or electricity. Those who reach it never return to this material world.**
**15.6**

## The Goal

Years ago, when my then boyfriend John and I first visited the ancient Indian holy town of Vrindavan, I was an atheist, and the spirituality of the place didn't interest me. But photographically its people were captivating. Beyond the rustic simplicity typical of Indian villagers, they had astounding faith in God – Krishna – and ongoing remembrance of Him. Passing each other – and me – on the cobblestone streets they would earnestly call out the name of Krishna's closest companion. Every street had temples, ceremonies and celebrations. Stores sold paraphernalia for worshiping Krishna; books revealed esoteric knowledge about Him. Old ladies sat together for hours daily to sing for His pleasure; children tending white cows played together while calling out His names. Old men meditated on Him on the banks of the sacred Yamuna River. Krishna and the love of His devotees were everywhere. In the course of seeing all this, at odd moments some invisible ornate gates briefly opened before me, divulging an intimate and charming but alien realm, a realm that enticed with a flourish of love. Then my cynicism would unleash and those gates would clang shut – with me outside, a journalist peering in to note the sublime.

Four months later, also in Vrindavan, John and I were married and for years, as we kept moving from city to city, our work and the reputation and prosperity we earned from it kept me aloof from spiritual goals. Mundane reasoning said that those goals were imaginary anyway, and I crowded my life with unending prosaic concerns and wasted my energy on the notably insignificant, pretending my bustling and harried activity gave it significance. Days and years frittered away in meaninglessness.

> What profiteth a man if he gains the whole world yet suffers the loss of his eternal soul?
>
> — Lord Jesus Christ

Eventually Bhaktivedanta Swami Prabhupada and Bhagavad-gita convinced me that failure means to be consumed with material gain and fame, which are useless to the *jivatma*, and success means to make spiritual progress, which lastingly benefits the *jivatma* and carries it toward the topmost goal.

> In this process there is no loss or diminution, and a little advancement on this path can save one from the greatest fear.
>
> — Bhagavad-gita 2.40

As humankind has (with minor cultural variations) a sense of a universal, objective moral law, so it also has a sense of an ultimate goal as beyond this mundane realm. Every belief system and religious tradition propounds a transcendent goal.

> In the Buddhist scriptures Lord Buddha advises that one achieve nirvana by giving up the materialistic way of life. In the Bible, which is also scripture, one will find the same advice: one should cease materialistic life and return to the kingdom of God. In any scripture one may examine, especially the Vedic scripture, the same advice is given: one should give up his materialistic life and return to his original, spiritual life.
>
> — Bhaktivedanta Swami Prabhupada

I'm meant to make spiritual strides, and when I try to do so, unforeseen and ecstatic changes happen: like the expression of faith that my family's and my life has become; like the sense of rootedness and belonging, of liberty and gladness that settled on me in Sharanagati (I'd longed for these feelings everywhere else we'd lived but never had them); like my unabashed happiness about little miracles – a bulb Priya and I planted makes extraordinarily complex, fragrant flowers with saffron-colored stamens that shoot out, dropping pollen on our altar; like the weather patterns John and I watch coming along the mountainsides from the south, bringing sunshine, wind, rain or snow; like my ponderings over all the things I could be but don't want to be doing elsewhere (what a luxury to have time to think, to read, to wonder!). Just as an impatient child who's been hiding from friends in a dank woodshed finally bursts

into the daylight bubbly with delight, so after a lifetime of sitting with musty misconceptions about identity and purpose, I've finally sprung, joyful, into a community of spiritually awake individuals.

In Sharanagati I have everything I want, I'm grateful for it all, and yet I'm also prodded by nostalgia: so much more awaits me that I can't imagine but can sense beyond my senses, beyond my mind and intelligence. After a day's pleasing labor I stand by my fence and smell and hear and see again the yawning stretch of land on which I strive for a home beyond my home, a home beyond all banal and petty goals.

Yet, this other home is not to so consume me that I neglect my earthly duties; on the contrary, I must try to fulfill them with excellence. The puzzle and transformative power of bhakti, devotional service to God, is that it enchants daily life by gracing it with such purpose and meaning that I'm delivered to God even as I go about my regular day.

Bhagavad-gita's message is sacred. God is real, His place is real, and His words, filling me with hope, offer the vibrant means of coming ever closer to Him and His place. Bhaktivedanta Swami Prabhupada writes, "be captivated by this information. Transfer yourself to that eternal world."

*We should live in such a way that we keep ourselves always healthy and strong in mind and intelligence so that we can distinguish the goal of life from a life full of problems.*

— Bhaktivedanta Swami Prabhupada

*We may not arrive at our port within a calculable period, but we would preserve the true course.*

— Henry David Thoreau

**The splendor of the sun, which dissipates the darkness of this whole world, comes from Me. And the splendor of the moon and the splendor of fire are also from Me. 15.12**

## The Greatness of God

In early May, modernity came to me in Sharanagati when John gave me an 80 GB iPod for my birthday. I downloaded all of Bhaktivedanta Swami Prabhupada's lectures onto it and spend an hour each day in our kayak, headphones on, gliding around Lake Sharanagati, wending through tall rushes on the lake's banks as Bhaktivedanta Swami speaks into my ears, presenting the culture he lived by. That culture embodies valor, integrity, etiquette, self-control and godliness, but I fail to feel its full weight. It's far easier for me to understand the slovenliness and weakness in me and in the world around me – evidenced by broken promises, ailing relationships and proliferating sorrow. What a world. And what zeal Bhaktivedanta Swami had to so boldly introduce a revolutionary culture centered on Bhagavad-gita. Although he was in the Western milieu, he was untinged by it; and his words, imbued with the power of his pure intent, make sense.

God and His energies, Bhaktivedanta Swami says, exceed my understanding. How can my five flawed senses, my limited intellect, my haphazard memory and my filters of preconceptions and assumptions possibly grasp He who transcends them all? In every way God surpasses me. So, in light of my tininess, I try to give up my arrogance and, surprisingly, am happy in my meekness before Him. As the sun glares down on me, I paddle steadily against the wind, awestruck by God's complete opulence and capability.

> One should meditate upon God as the one who knows everything, as He who is the oldest, who is the controller, who is smaller than

> the smallest, who is the maintainer of everything, who is beyond all material conception, who is inconceivable, and who is always a person. He is luminous like the sun, and He is transcendental, beyond this material nature.
>
> — Bhagavad-gita 8.9

In any situation, painful or joyful, I can offer my homage to God and ask "What is the lesson in this for me?" And I can relax, knowing that as my layers of conditioning peel away and my enthusiasm to become a better person increases, God will help me. To Him, each person is precious; yet another aspect of His greatness is His all-inclusive, responsive love.

> As all surrender unto Me, I reward them accordingly.
>
> — Bhagavad-gita 4.11, Krishna speaking

Patiently engaging my senses, emotions and intellect in bhakti will let me experience God. By the quintessential spiritual activity, bhakti, the inconceivable allows Himself to be conceived. Of all of His unlimited greatnesses, the potency God puts in bhakti is the greatest.

> Only by undivided devotional service [bhakti] can I be understood as I am ... Only in this way can you enter into the mysteries of My understanding.
>
> — Bhagavad-gita 11.54, Krishna speaking

My kayak hour is over. I've been all around the lake and now, returning to the dock, optimism saturates me.

*Not by the senses, by the mind, by the life air, by thoughts within the heart, or by the vibration of words can the living entities ascertain the real situation of God.*

— Srimad-Bhagavatam 6.3.16

*How can the mind conceive of God who is beyond material conceptions and without material qualities? The mind can perceive God by the power of bhakti arising from the mercy of God.*

— Visvanath Chakravarti Thakur

*Let us accept truth, even when it surprises us and alters our views.*

— George Sand

**I am seated in everyone's heart, and from Me come remembrance, knowledge and forgetfulness. 15.15**

## Remembrance, Knowledge and Forgetfulness

My conscience, the voice within that tells me not to lie, steal or harm, that tells me to be tolerant and helpful, is the voice of Paramatma – God in my heart. He witnesses my activities, He lets me do what I want, but, as my most dear friend, He also nudges me with feelings of uneasiness and guilt or, at other times, with feelings of inner approval and "rightness." Internal conflict is my desire colliding with His. He begs me to follow the directions of the scriptures and saints; I beg to differ.

> Suppose you are going to do something that is not very good. The conscience is beating, "No, no, you should not do this. You should not do this." Without the sanction of the Supreme, I cannot do anything, so if I persist then the sanction is given, "At your own risk." God does not sanction you to do anything criminal. But if I persistently want to do something criminal, then God sanctions it, "All right, do it at your own risk."
>
> — Bhaktivedanta Swami Prabhupada

I've always had a mysterious inkling of a benevolent force near me, a muse of some sort, but it was the Bhagavad-gita's forthright information, consistent and logical, which demystified the inner guide.

Many years ago when my family and I were still living in our Los Angeles apartment, we could have squelched our pervasive dissatisfaction and stayed there, or we could have moved practically anywhere. On a grand scale, where we moved was a miniscule decision, but it was momentous for us and we suffered weeks of indecision. One option was Sharanagati, but I was afraid of such a new lifestyle; clinging to the old one was safer. Confused and disturbed, John and I twisted, turned and flip-flopped, and then relaxed the urgency of our need to decide. We waited, living temporarily in the realm of "I don't know," in a fertile uncertainty, where we hoped Paramatma would have the space to give us direction in the form of clear intelligence. We read the scriptures, kept company with God's servants and asked them – saintly people – their opinion, all the while trying to understand what was best. Did we do the right thing by settling in the tundra of Sharanagati? Time – another form of God – will let us know with more certainty, but as of now, yes. John and I are spiritually nourished here and our daughter loves it.

Bhagavad-gita opens me to options and gives me knowledge to help discern between them. Through Bhagavad-gita I realize why my repeated attempts to enjoy the temporal have been frustrated; I realize that if anything I learn or do makes me feel superior to someone else, I have misunderstood; and I realize that I don't have to impress anyone – the very idea is ludicrous. I simply need to remember who I am.

God is wonderful and, inconceivably, He takes the essence of my devotion, overlooks my faults and reciprocates whatever little love I may have. Dogma and fanaticism, intolerance and exclusivism are not part of His world, but are due only to my forgetfulness of Him. Gently, like the coming of daylight, I grow to love the Gita's uncomplicated truths – truths that may well be the most poignant of all.

*God is the original Supersoul, the father of all living entities. Consequently there are no impediments to pleasing Him or worshiping Him under any conditions. The relationship between the* jivatma *and the Supreme Person is always a fact, and therefore there is no difficulty in pleasing the Lord.*

— Srimad-Bhagavatam 7.6.19

*According to one's attitude, Krishna becomes one's direct advisor or Krishna becomes unknown. This is not Krishna's partiality; it is His response to one's ability to understand Him.*

— Bhaktivedanta Swami Prabhupada

*The Almighty has His own purposes.*

— Abraham Lincoln

**Satisfaction, simplicity, gravity, self-control and purification of one's existence are the austerities of the mind. 17.16**

## My Goodness! – Austerity

When I accepted the spiritual path, my spiritual teacher had me make five simple vows: that I would refrain from illicit sex, intoxication, gambling and non-vegetarian food, and that I would chant God's names each day. Swept up in the flush of the moment, I didn't fully consider the gravity of these lifelong austerities. After all, I was young and knew almost everything.

A short time later I lived near a Krishna temple and every morning well before dawn would attend the first worship of the day along with a few other stalwarts. Our little group quickly became insufferably insolent.

"Why are we the only ones here every time? Where's everyone else?"

"The others are cozy under their quilts, that's where. They have late night get-togethers and can't get up early."

"Shall we play the instruments louder so they at least turn over in their sleep?"

My spirit grew heavy, my mind stiffened with sanctimony, and the distance between me and those I love widened. A lush, thorny tangle of pride left me feeling awful.

Yet, despite the ill effect it had on me, austerity – rising early and following rules and regulations – is necessary for my spiritual well-being. Without austerity feverish gusts of desires will blow me around helplessly in a world littered with dissatisfaction. Austerity puts me, the *jivatma* – not the mind's mood swings, the compulsions of passion or the demands of fashion – in control. By the vigor it gives me I can honor my priorities and keep my commitments.

> Nothing is possible without austerity.... The more we engage in austerities, the more we become powerful by the grace of God.
>
> — Bhaktivedanta Swami Prabhupada

Provocative vows of morality strip away the darkness that shrouds me – a *jivatma,* an ember that glows deep within. A saccharine religion that doesn't discriminate between moral and immoral behavior, that lets me do whatever I like, won't impact my spiritual life.

> Propaganda that one can enjoy this life materially and at the same time spiritually advance is simply bogus.
>
> — Bhaktivedanta Swami Prabhupada

Avoidance of the immoral and acceptance of the moral is nothing to be proud of; it's simply normality. And following the rules and regulations of normality are my response to a pure summons whose secret is perceived through emotion and intuition as well as through reason. So, I do my day-to-day tasks with attention to what I'm doing, not on what others are or are not doing, and the flow of my Sharanagati life fills my soul with long echoes of harmony. In a moment of deep feeling, as the dazzle of afternoon light settles on me in dappled splendor, I grasp that the simple austerities I've accepted are the best way to live.

> Even if one does not accept God, His instructions are so exalted and beneficial for humanity that if one follows His instructions one will be saved.
>
> — Bhaktivedanta Swami Prabhupada

Done gently, austerity yields the succulent fruits of gladness, of warmth, of lightness, of excitement. It slowly unfolds a life in which I am not an isolated individual but part of a great tradition that's moving toward transcendence. Life with austerity is a communion with sages of yore where I quietly harvest a certain deep happiness that never leaves me whatever my fate. Austerity's melodies rouse me to frolic with the mystery of spirit.

*Without sacrifice one can never live happily on this planet or in this life: what then of the next?*

— Bhagavad-gita 4.31

*Live simply. Love generously. Care deeply. Speak kindly. Leave the rest to God.*

— Old farmer's adage

**From the beginning of creation, the three words om tat sat were used to indicate God and were chanted for the satisfaction of God. 17.23**

## Freedom

When my family and I left Sharanagati to stay in Mumbai for some months, our daughter was reading one of the Harry Potter

books. Halfway around the world, the two Mumbai sisters who became her good friends were reading from the same series, and together they – and the sisters' parents – watched Harry Potter films. (The books were better, they all decided.)

Like my daughter, her friends, her friends' parents, and billions of others throughout the world and throughout the ages, I'm also drawn to otherworldly domains where clever, courageous beings act in astonishing ways. Fiction doesn't come out of nowhere but is derived from aspects of fact. Fictitious stories about unperceived worlds and our attraction to those stories is due to our subconscious awareness that such worlds actually exist in some form – although perhaps not as depicted. But, due to who we are, we're captivated by such stories.

> The need of the spirit soul is that he wants to get out of the limited sphere of material bondage and fulfill his desire for complete freedom. He wants to get out of the covered walls of the greater universe. He wants to see the free light and the spirit.
>
> — Bhaktivedanta Swami Prabhupada

Thus through the ages people everywhere are attracted to stories that explore otherworldly realms. And the ultimate of all otherworldly realms is divine. There, according to our desire, we relate with God as a servant, a friend, a parent or even a lover, enjoying exchanges that sometimes include humor, wonder, chivalry, compassion, fear and even loving anger. Entering this divine dimension, however, is not as easy as entering a fictional world.

> Those who meditate on Me as the Supreme Person, their minds constantly engaged in remembering Me, undeviated from the path, they are sure to reach Me.
>
> — Bhagavad-gita 8.8, Krishna speaking

God and His realm are beyond my perception, but just as I daily water my garden, eat my home-grown vegetables and go for walks, so I also defect from this earthly culture where faith is placed only in what's perceivable. I live my own spiritual life, saying my own "yes" and "no" and not merely echoing the answers of a mundane system. My choices are not clean-cut and final, but involve me in tension, in tendency. I keep on choosing one way and also have the freedom to choose the opposite way. At any time my family and I could pack up and leave Sharanagati, take up residence elsewhere and deal with the pleasures and difficulties of that new life. And we also have the freedom to stay put, to let our roots penetrate and gather strength from nourishment below the surface of events. Ultimately the freedom of satisfaction is inside me, waiting to be tapped. Flitting from place to place like a frightened starling may actually not be from my free choice but from the force of my dissatisfaction, from my restlessness.

Freedom can mean stretching my wings and taking flight on an inward journey toward bhakti, the dynamic divine force of the *jivatma*. Whatever I may be, if I transcend pretensions, daily try to commune with God's civilization and am satisfied with His blessings, I'll be free. In the final analysis, satisfying God evokes my satisfaction and my freedom.

Spiritual life is not complicated. Although I make uncountable mistakes, although I repeatedly fail and try again to improve, my spiritual satisfaction and the freedom that accompanies it are part of who I am – part of my identity – and as such are incorruptible. Eternally. I simply need to remember this and to claim these qualities as my own.

*Deliberate on this fully, and then do what you wish to do.*
— Bhagavad-gita 18.63, Krishna speaking

**The place of action [the body], the doer, the various senses, the many different kinds of endeavor, and ultimately the Supersoul – these are the five factors of action. 18.14**

## Action

I – a *jivatma* – am the doer, and for every action I do I have one driving motivation and ultimate goal: to be happy. Actually, by my nature as a *jivatma* I'm already happy yet, dominated and distracted by my body and senses, my innate happiness is mostly covered. There is, however, a natural activity that uncovers this innate happiness: service done with love.

> We can see that one friend serves another friend, the mother serves the son, the wife serves the husband, the husband serves the wife and so on. If we go on searching in this spirit, it will be seen that there is no exception in the society of living beings to the activity of service. The politician presents his manifesto for the public to convince them of his capacity for service. The voters therefore give the politician their valuable votes, thinking that he will render valuable service to society. The shopkeeper serves

> the customer, and the artisan serves the capitalist. The capitalist serves the family, and the family serves the state ... In this way we can see that no living being is exempt from rendering service to other living beings, and therefore we can safely conclude that service is the constant companion of the living being and that the rendering of service is the eternal religion of the living being.
>
> — Bhaktivedanta Swami Prabhupada

Bhakti is service free of the desire to control another or to gain possessions; it is devotional service done with remembrance of God and done for His pleasure. Bhakti is happiness. It is the relationship between the whole – God, who resides in every living thing – and the part, *jivatma* – every one of us. Bhakti is the *jivatmas'* action in harmony with God and with each other.

> Bhakti-yoga teaches us the science of loving every one of the living entities perfectly by the easy method of loving Krishna.... If

> we learn how to love Krishna, then it is very easy to immediately and simultaneously love every living being. It is like pouring water on the root of a tree or supplying food to one's stomach.
>
> — Bhaktivedanta Swami Prabhupada

When we Sharanagati-ites get together, we let bhakti form the basis of our closeness, of our reciprocation and of the honor we give to each individual. Sitting in a circle on the lakeside dock for our weekly singing get-together, this time under a sparkling sky on a September evening, a few of us take turns leading. When Priya's turn comes, she plays the harmonium, her youthful voice rising over the lapping waves, and we respond, chanting the names of God in chorus. To our north the mountains are engraved with long rows of ridges and vales as if someone's huge, slightly spread fingers made deep scratches in the earth, the wound now covered by dense forests of firs. Final rays of sunlight stream overhead, and the shadow of the western mountains creeps up and over the eastern ridge. The lake's reeds bend under a steady breeze, then the sun is gone and we zip up our jackets. I reflect for a moment. Because God is just, I know I'm safe; unlike man-made justice, His justice is meant to bring me closer to Him. Because God is compassionate, I know I'm loved. And when I trust His omnipresence, when I try to please Him and am not attached to the outcome of my actions, I've placed myself in His hands just as much as I have now placed myself in a valley protected by His mountain ranges. I accept that He knows things that I do not.

It's only 8 p.m., but the wind has become unfriendly and in the dimness we head home, united by bhakti, action for God who is Himself the wellspring of harmony.

*One thing I do know: the only ones among you who will be really happy are those who have sought and found how to serve.*

— Albert Schweitzer

**By worship of God, who is the source of all beings and who is all-pervading, one can attain perfection through performing one's own work. 18.46**

## Work

One spring, I filled half a garden bed with seed potatoes and happily harvested a large potato crop the following fall. The next spring, however, I was surprised to see green potato shoots coming up from the same bed. I had thought it was empty and had planned to leave it fallow, but accidentally I'd left a few potatoes in the ground. They'd survived the winter and were now volunteering. I put compost on them, watered and weeded them and, months later, on a bright October morning, harvested them. That same afternoon I cut a few up, boiled them in a small amount of water, added a touch of salt and served them as part of our lunch. John tried them first.

"You put a lot of butter in these potatoes."

"No, I didn't put any at all."

"You're kidding."

"No, really. Maybe they taste buttery because they're fresh."

"Amazing."

When I ate them I thought the same thing John had – they tasted astonishingly buttery. I considered all the plastic-wrapped supermarket

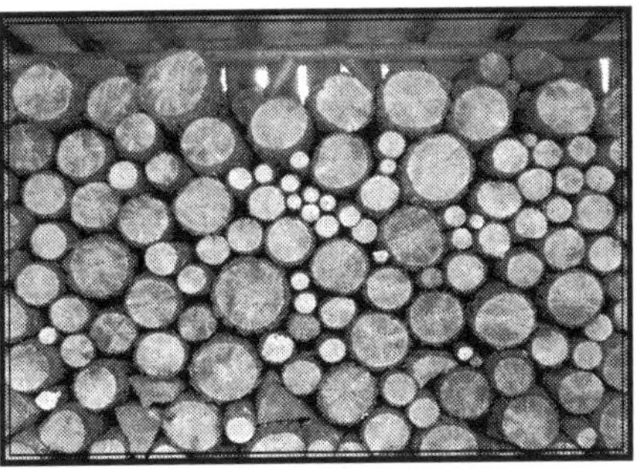

potatoes that I'd bought over many years and realized that I didn't really know what a potato tasted like. I thought how supermarket vegetables were who-knows-how-old and shipped from who-knows-where, and how I had to work like a cog in a vast, relentless economic machine to afford them – as well as to afford so many other questionable products. My whole life, I thought, has been cog-like. I've been waiting in traffic jams or tearing down highways at dangerous speeds to get to who-knows-how-many questionable destinations. The dullness of that life, with its constant pressure of pointless activity, deadened and debased me. And now, with dirt under my nails and grass stains on my knees, I can say that I will no longer bow down to an altar of money, of status, of public opinion or of common nonsense. I refuse to endlessly shop and fret.

On the strength of Bhagavad-gita's and my teacher's words, I take it that my dissatisfaction with mundane life is due to my identity as *jivatma*. Slowly, I'm emerging from my personal plastic wrapping and adding spiritual intent to my work.

> Work done as a sacrifice for God has to be performed; otherwise work causes bondage in this material world. Therefore perform your prescribed duties for His satisfaction, and in that way you will always remain free from bondage.
>
> — Bhagavad-gita 3.9

> The only distinction between materialistic activity and spiritual activity is that material activity is performed only to satisfy one's own senses whereas spiritual activity is meant to satisfy the transcendental senses of God.
>
> — Bhaktivedanta Swami Prabhupada

John and I could have applied Bhagavad-gita's teachings to our jobs and activities in Los Angeles – it doesn't matter what work one does or where one does it; all work is glorious if it's done in a spirit of bhakti, devotion to God. City facilities are also God's and can be used in His service.

> A man working in Krishna consciousness in a factory does not associate himself with the work of the factory, nor with the workers of the factory. He simply works for Krishna. And when he gives up the result for Krishna, he is acting transcendentally.
>
> — Bhaktivedanta Swami Prabhupada

In my case, however, city life was a struggle to survive and self-realization was another struggle – for eternal life. I thought it better to have one struggle rather than two. City allurements are designed to entangle and to weaken willpower, and city living creates gnawing pragmatism and grumpy perfunctoriness that can dismay a spiritual seeker.

Sharanagati's open-air simplicity allures me toward bhakti's impenetrable mysteries, and this valley seems designed to let me feel the deep satisfaction bhakti offers. In imponderable spaciousness I can more easily align my heart and mind with who I am; I can more easily dedicate my work to God; I can more easily depend on Him for the results; and I can feel happy just from trying to do these things. Here I gain confidence in the simple means God has given me for reaching Him – remembering Him while working for Him – and, relying on His mercy, I'm inspired as never before.

John edits videos, I write, and other Sharanagati residents work as carpenters, craftspeople, counselors, handymen, housewives, teachers, therapists, secretaries, soap makers, organic farmers and vegetarian cooks; the largest family among us owns and operates the local health food and gift store.

> Everyone should be allowed to render service to the Lord to the best of his ability, and everyone should appreciate the service

of others. Since everyone is a servant, everyone is on the same platform and is allowed to serve God according to his ability.

— Bhaktivedanta Swami Prabhupada

We residents live as simply and as wisely as we're able, and we maintain ourselves without difficulty. Daily, the sense of connection that work done for God readily awards, knits us together. The quiet rhythms of our spiritual practice anchor us so well that sometimes it's hard to remember that life had ever been otherwise.

Week after week, year after year, bit by bit, the work we do for God and His servants transforms us. Layers of false ambition, unneeded possessions, shallowness, pride and defensiveness fall away. We become more true to ourselves knowing that each act we do for the pleasure of God and His servants is meaningful, each thought of Him important, each relationship involving Him significant. When we work for God our consciousness expands to encompass exalted secrets that stretch us to be more than we thought we could be and that give us more than we imagined existed. Working for God is a form of love that reveals timeless joy.

*This knowledge is the king of education, the most secret of all secrets. It is the purest knowledge, and since it gives direct perception of the self by realization, it is the perfection of religion. It is everlasting, and it is joyfully performed.*

— Bhagavad-gita 9.2

*Without love, the outward work is of no value; but whatever is done out of love, be it ever so little, is wholly fruitful. For God regards the greatness of the love that prompts a man, rather than the greatness of his achievement.*

— Thomas à Kempis

*Cooperation pleases God and He shows His pleasure by synergy – He makes our combined effort greater than the sum of our individual efforts.*

— Varsana Swami

**One who is transcendentally situated at once realizes God and becomes fully joyful. That person never laments or desires anything material and is equally disposed toward every living entity. Such a person attains bhakti – devotional service – to Me.**
**18.54**

## Joy

As part of God I am, like Him, joyful. I access this transcendent joy not through sensual indulgence or mental speculation, but by accepting the impermanence of everything worldly and the permanence of God, of the *jivatma* and of their delightful relationship of love.

> Just as a deer, because of ignorance, cannot see the water within a well covered by grass, but runs after water elsewhere, the *jivatma* covered by the material body does not see the happiness within itself, but runs after happiness in the material world.
> — Srimad-Bhagavatam 7.13.29

By making me aware of my identity beyond my body and mind, Bhagavad-gita makes me a renegade from flickering joy. I begin to cast off the hundreds and thousands of mundane desires that are like nooses around my neck, dragging me to a sad, shallow life burdened by unnecessary disappointment. And, as I begin to realize that no one and nothing can even slightly alter the radiance of who I am, I'm humbled by my predicament in this world. My eagerness for the privilege of divine service increases.

> When shall I engage as Your permanent, eternal servant and always feel joyful to have such a fitting master?
> — Chaitanya Charitamrita 2.1.206

I think I will be joyful when I am the master, but joy comes from bhakti, devotional service to the true Master. I think I will be joyful when I am invulnerable, but joy comes from accepting my vulnerability before Him. I think I'll be joyful when my demands and expectations are met, but joy comes when I'm no longer dependent upon things being a certain way; when I stop resisting God's will and see nothing outside the scope of His control.

We in Sharanagati have discovered that it is possible to have the habit of happiness. Not all of us are known for smiles and laughter – in my case, quite the opposite – but within us healthy seedlings of spiritual hope thrive. This attitude may not be constant – we're forgetful at times – but it's unrelated to circumstances and evinced by lives of kindness and confidence. On occasion I travel, and when I mention our Canadian home to the people I meet, invariably they say, "Aren't the winters horrible up there?" Yes, the winters are long, dark and cold. Yet for a number of Sharanagati residents it's our favorite season. We use those four tranquil months as a silent tuning fork, a focused, undisturbed time when we can refine our inner life and embolden its beautiful melodies. Even winters, when diamond like sparks of sunlight gambol on the snow, can surprise us with joy.

Joy arises when I accept my present circumstance as an arrangement by God due to my own past acts, when I refrain from whining about my troubles, and when I trust that God, my well-wisher, will one day be mine.

> The pure devotee is always within the core of My heart, and I am always in the heart of the pure devotee. My devotees do not know anything else but Me, and I do not know anyone else but them.
> — Srimad-Bhagavatam 9.4.68, Krishna speaking

Joy comes when I don't strive for it – when it's not my goal but the unintended side-effect of my dedication to an authentic purpose beyond myself. By seeing God throughout His creation I feel love for my fellow creatures, overlook their weaknesses and take joy in their small and great qualities.

In joy we live contentedly without the self-consciousness that makes us constantly compare ourselves to others to see how big we are. We work and love selflessly, without needing special recognition. Fortified by joy, we become far greater than the things that happen to us. Despite reverses we go on.

The spiritual joy of bhakti makes us generous, lively, bold, and unaffected by mundane wrangling and the accumulation or loss of objects and money. This joy, which is available to anyone, augments our awareness of the balance, order and rhythm around us. It's a state of consciousness on a plane beyond time that can be attained now.

> The thoughts of My devotees dwell in Me, their lives are fully devoted to My service, and they derive great satisfaction and bliss from always enlightening one another and conversing about Me.
> — Bhagavad-gita 10.9, Krishna speaking

As I increase my present moment of awareness of people, the environment, the circumstances, the opportunity and use my time for bhakti, I feel childlike wonder in simple things. Walking through our valley to the temple, to my friends' homes, to meetings, to use the school's internet and just for the simple pleasure of walking, no traffic drone dulls my perception, no pavement hardens my steps. The earth beneath my feet and the enchantment of the dark forests welcome me like old friends. I hear ducks hiding in the dense reeds around our funny-shaped lake. I watch the teenagers bend forward on their horses and laugh in glee as they canter down a country road. As I walk I don't force thoughts into or out of my mind, but softly chant God's names, fingering my rosary like beads, feeling strong and lighthearted and at peace with the world. Despite my many shortcomings, my spirit soars. "This is the day which the Lord hath made; we will rejoice and be glad in it." (Psalm 118:24)

Joy is in becoming worthy of God's gift of bhakti, and joy is the effect of being touched by this gift.

> God is prepared to give bhakti-yoga to everyone, but we must be capable of receiving it. That is the secret.
>
> — Bhaktivedanta Swami Prabhupada

Joy is the awakening of the higher nature of each individual. Discovering my permanent, spiritual self through the wisdom of Bhagavad-gita, I pray to become grateful to guru and God, for without humble gratitude all knowledge and spiritual striving are so much mental clutter and pompous verbiage. Just knowing about *jivatma's* joy gives me fresh impetus for this path.

A heart that is, even partially, absorbed in Bhagavad-gita is gentled and gradually comes to feel the fullness of genuine joy – a joy that isn't susceptible to the winds of time or to material calamities. If I only realized how great this joy is, I would try for it with the utmost attention.

*One can understand Me as I am, as God, the Supreme Person, only by bhakti. And when one is in full consciousness of Me by such bhakti, that person can enter into the kingdom of God.*

— Bhagavad-gita 18.55, Krishna speaking

*A living entity becomes established in spiritual, blissful life when he fully understands that his happiness depends on spiritual self-realization, which is the basic principle of bliss, and when he is eternally situated in the service of God, who has no other God above Him.*

— Taittiriya Upanisad 2.7

*Devotees should always be happy with all the dealings of their master, God. A devotee may be put into difficulty or opulence, but he should accept both as gifts of God and jubilantly engage in the service of God in all circumstances.*

— Bhaktivedanta Swami Prabhupada

*The joy of bhakti is experienced to the degree we are selfless in our efforts.*

— Radhanatha Swami

**If you become conscious of Me, you will pass over all the obstacles of conditioned life by My grace. If, however, you do not work in such consciousness but act through false ego, not hearing Me, you will be lost. 18.58**

## Harmony

As a tree's branches connect to its trunk, as musical instruments harmonize in a symphony, as seasonings meld in a stew, as colors form a rainbow, as flowers and leaves and ferns combine to make a

striking vase, so there's a common, harmonizing element underlying every race, religion and civilization. The bodies and minds of all people differ, yet all are *jivatmas*. I am one of those *jivatmas*, and harmony is natural to me, just as joy is. This harmony transcends theories, laws and doctrines; it's immovably established by my own direct inner comprehension of God and His integral parts, the *jivatmas*.

We Sharanagati residents come from all over – Canada, the U.S., England, Italy, Russia, India, Israel, Poland, Pakistan, Australia, Argentina, South Africa – and have different belief backgrounds. We were atheist, Christian, Catholic, Protestant, Hindu, Jewish and Muslim – yet we live in harmony.

One warm June evening in 2009 I said to John, "It's been ten years since we moved to Sharanagati. Do you think we did the right thing?"

"Yeah, we did. It feels like home here. It's a wonder we've stayed so long."

"Why do you think it worked?"

"I like that we create our own electricity and pipe in our own water. It feels right. At least we're a little self-sufficient. And I like that we're in a good community. But then again, we're so far from the airport!"

I felt the same way (even about the airport). A strong, soothing feeling of wholeness and empowerment wells up in me from living self-sufficiently in a community of people who are united despite their diversity. Ultimately, all of us – all *jivatmas* – have one Father, God.

As members of His extensive family, we are magnificently one. At the same time, because each of us – each *jivatma* – is a singular, inimitable individual, this family is beautifully diverse. I'm increasingly eager to wake up from my slumber and get to know my family members.

Each *jivatma* has a personal, unique, life-giving, reciprocally affectionate relationship with God and with other *jivatmas*. The whole world becomes more interesting when, without expectations, we are well-wishers of other *jivatmas*, and when we receive with joy whatever good wishes they give us. But even if another's affection for us is lacking, we can still remain an affectionate well-wisher of that person.

Affection for the *jivatma*, the spiritual soul, is itself spiritual and sacred. Love and affection create a unity whose embrace overlooks differences. And it's this love and affection – reciprocated or not – that completes me and makes irrelevant the empty proposals of nihilism, fanaticism, terrorism, racism, enmity and bias. Affection transcends disharmony. Affection creates harmony.

Bhagavad-gita's timely and timeless message of harmony is a river that flows through the parched lands of secularism and warring religions. Those who drink its clear water are deeply nourished. By the courtesy, justice and love that accompany that nourishment, they live in harmony.

*Only because of ignorance do people concoct differences and dualities.*

— Srimad-Bhagavatam 8.12.8

*The entire cosmic harmony is a settled fact by the will of the Supreme. So we must find the supreme will in every action of the cosmic situation. The human life is an opportunity to understand this cosmic harmony ... If you can grasp the direct meaning of Bhagavad-gita it will be possible to understand the basic principle of cosmic harmony.*

— Bhaktivedanta Swami Prabhupada

**As I repeatedly recall this wondrous and holy dialogue between Krishna and Arjuna, I take pleasure, being thrilled at every moment. 18.76**

## Thrilled at Every Moment

Bhagavad-gita does not promise sudden spiritual or material success. It is a lifelong guide for gradual inner improvement.

Such improvement may come erratically and without drama. After early insightful and enthusiastic phases, mistakes, misfortune, bad moods and pettiness can draw a heavy curtain between God and us, threatening our new-found direction. We may feel like forgetting Bhagavad-gita and living exclusively in the world of externals where scientific knowledge and technological know-how reign supreme. In Sharanagati some of our teenagers become restless after they graduate high school. They find work in Vancouver or some other city, but when they visit us, how much they appreciate having grown up here and the life they left behind! Some of these young people have gotten married, had children of their own and returned to Sharanagati to raise their children here. A new generation is finding that a community of like-minded people may be the best place to meet the challenges of spiritual progress; now three generations live in and are taking responsibility for the future of this unique valley.

Material knowledge cannot answer our questions about meaning and purpose and coherence. Mundane expertise has shaped us, entertained us, made us comfortable and left us in disarray. All its information and inventions could not grant us the elusive quality of fulfillment. We long to discover the world beyond the visible, and we do not want glib formulas, naïve beliefs or a pretense of certainty. Neither do we want to become hardened by skepticism and irreverence. So, we try to live both with our modern ways as well as with our inner awareness of a divine order, relying on Bhagavad-gita to raise the curtain between us and unseen aspects of reality. Sharanagati's school has eight computer stations, its residents use laptops and some have internet access; in our home we have normal trappings. Modern conveniences may save time, help us stay healthy and enhance our service. It's this service attitude, which is the essential quality of the *jivatma*, that dovetails material things for spiritual benefit.

By dovetailing matter to spirit, a world of the invisible, of forces and laws and relations beyond our present comprehension, awaits us through the Gita's verses. We approach those 700 short verses with reverent attentiveness and with a prayer-filled readiness to receive what they slowly yield. We linger, deliberate, re-read, reflect, and expect only that our humble effort may be pleasing to the speaker of those words. As we become receptive to His divine song, we become enchanted by it, its ageless wisdom always fresh and ready to yield unexpected riches. We mine it again and again.

As the greedy see everything as a source of money, as the lusty see everything as conducive to sex, so those who are alert to Bhagavad-gita see cause and purpose behind everything. With an open mind and a willingness to surrender to the process of bhakti, they admit God's guidance into their lives and act upon that guidance. They are gradually transformed: they grow in awareness, in sensitivity, in the ability to love and to be themselves. Their negative feelings are gradually replaced with positive ones; they turn monotony, suffering and even disaster into sources of strength.

Karma, reincarnation and the modes of nature are realities that affect us all. Yet there is much that we will never fully know. God is in the world, is in us and is at liberty to do as He pleases. If He so desires, He may remain hidden. When He does things His way, not ours, we accept His will and freely cooperate with Him. Whatever happens or does not happen is His decision. We act with valor, shun complacency, appreciate His grace, and avoid making demands of Him.

Through Bhagavad-gita we find what is most rare – God, the Supreme Person: real, concrete and intimate, full of energy, fun-loving, always young, always beautiful, always attracting our hearts with His charm and tremendous mystery.

And as a fragmental part of Him, the eternal, radiant *jivatma* has His qualities minutely. It is aware and alert, respectful, energetic in all its tasks, filled with joy and exuberance, content, grateful and wondrous. It sees the dignity of people and the value of things.

Knowing our identity, we live to serve and to share in a community. Each person is their own genius and it's a pleasure simply to pay attention to them. They enrich our lives with new vistas. We find pleasure in trying to help them. We care deeply and focus fully on them, yet we let them be themselves. We praise their genius and see it blossom while we flourish in our own calling. We Sharanagati residents get together regularly: Tuesday evenings for women's meetings where we exchange thoughts and initiate community events; Wednesdays some of us read the scriptures together, discussing, asking questions and sharing insights; Friday evenings a big group gathers to taste the power of meditating on God's names; Saturdays Sharanagati-ites fill up our small house and, by candlelight and while I serve out hot herbal tea, everyone who wants to – including the children – leads the singing of God's names to the melody and tempo of their choice; Sundays we gather at the temple to discuss Bhagavad-gita, sing, dance and feast on food that's been offered to God. On special festival days we have parades, plays, skits, musicals, dances, choruses, puppet and talent shows. And each day we can celebrate our spiritual journey.

Rejoicing in the whole process of bhakti we discover with relief that to be profoundly happy we do not have to own or control or be especially distinguished.

God is great, I am small, and by His grace I can humbly serve Him. Duties done honestly, pain and suffering accepted graciously, friendship with our fellows, the conviction that God values us all equally and wants the best for all of us, the certainty that we can fit in His scheme and render bhakti with body, mind and words – these create joys that we had never even imagined and that no amount of fame or fortune could replicate.

An inconceivable, all-inclusive design connects each created thing to the other in an incredibly complex web of interdependence. Concealed within the intricacies and beauty and brilliance of the creation is unity underlying opposites, accord amid contradictions, and oneness in differences. Offering bhakti to the Supreme Designer for His pleasure evokes His invaluable reciprocation: transcendence touches our intelligence and ecstasy is included in our sense control. We perceive the greatness we are individually capable of and, through all the vicissitudes of our outward life, in the depths of our being we remain joyful.

*Just go for walks, live in peace, let change come quietly and invisibly on the inside.*

— Thomas Merton

*God does not die on the day when we cease to believe in a personal deity, but we die on the day when our lives cease to be illuminated by the steady radiance, renewed daily, of a wonder, the source of which is beyond all reason.*

— Dag Hammarskjold

*Every spot on earth where discourses on God are held is a place of pilgrimage.*

— Bhaktisiddhanta Sarasvati Thakur

# Epilogue

Every morning in Los Angeles, when I drove our daughter to her nursery school a mile from our apartment, I passed six traffic lights, five stops signs, two shopping centers, a meat-packing plant, dozens of billboards and innumerable cars. In Sharanagati, when the weather permits, my daughter and I bicycle to her school along three miles of dirt roads that wind near a lake and through a forest. On the way we pass the homes of our friends. When the weather's bad, I drive her on the "main" road – also dirt – and we pass horses, ducks, swans, grazing cows, occasional bears and coyotes and, infrequently, another car. As we go we watch the rising light of the sun create rainbows on the frosted pine needles. Sometimes the mist is as thick as potato soup; other days sunlight pours into our eyes so brightly that we can't see.

Here, the ponderous mountains, the silent spaciousness, the crisp air have replaced stifling urban stress and pettiness. Here, we chase away sameness and boredom by abandoning ourselves to song and dance; we laugh easily at our many failings. Here, we wonder and delight in the Supreme Person who is behind everything, and feel deeply thankful to Him. Here, everything is connected – as it could be anywhere – through bhakti. We breathe deeply the delicate fragrances of this connection; we welcome its gentle melodies and its embrace of harmony.

*Wherever there is Krishna, the master of all mystics, and wherever there is Arjuna, the supreme archer, there will also certainly be opulence, victory, extraordinary power and morality.*

— Bhagavad-gita 18.78

# Glossary

**Arjuna**—an intimate friend and eternal associate of Krishna. Krishna took the role of his chariot driver and spoke the Bhagavad-gita to him.

**Bhagavad-gita**—a record of a conversation between Lord Krishna and His disciple, Arjuna. In its 700 verses the Gita summarizes all knowledge about the soul, God, dharma, sacrifice, austerity, charity, yoga, karma, reincarnation, time, material nature and bhakti.

**bhakti**—devotional service to the Supreme Personality of Godhead, Krishna, untinged by sense gratification or philosophical speculation.

**Bhaktisiddhanta Sarasvati Thakur**—(1874-1936) the spiritual master of Bhaktivedanta Swami Prabhupada and a powerful preacher who founded sixty four missions in India.

**Bhakti Tirtha Swami**—(1950-2005) a disciple of Bhaktivedanta Swami Prabhupada who served as a specialist in international relations and conflict resolution and who wrote extensively on those topics.

**Bhaktivedanta Swami Prabhupada**—(1896-1977) His Divine Grace A. C. Bhaktivedanta Swami Prabhupada, a disciple of Bhaktisiddhanta Sarasvati Thakur. He is the tenth generation from Sri Chaitanya and the founder-acharya of the International Society for Krishna Consciousness (ISKCON). Bhaktivedanta Swami Prabhupada was a widely-acclaimed author of more than seventy books on the science of bhakti-yoga, unalloyed Krishna consciousness, and the world's most distinguished teacher of Vedic religion and thought. He worked incessantly to spread Krishna consciousness all over the world. Under his guidance his society grew into a worldwide confederation of hundreds of ashrams, schools, temples, institutes and farm communities.

**Bhaktivinode Thakur**—(1838-1914) the father of Bhaktisiddhanta Sarasvati Thakur, the grand-spiritual master of His Divine Grace A. C. Bhaktivedanta Swami Prabhupada and a great spiritual teacher.

**bhakti-yoga**—the process of devotional service to the Supreme Personality of Godhead, Krishna.

**B. R. Sridhar Swami**—(1895-1988) a prominent disciple of Bhakti-siddhanta Sarasvati Thakur.

**Chaitanya Bhagavat**—a biography of Sri Chaitanya's early life by Vrindavan das Thakur (1507-1589).

**Chaitanya Charitamrita**—the authorized biography of Sri Chaitanya written in the late sixteenth century by Krishna das Kaviraj Goswami.

**Chanakya Pandit**—an advisor to King Chandragupta and a famous author of books containing aphorisms on politics and morality.

***japa***—the soft recitation of Krishna's holy names: Hare Krishna Hare Krishna, Krishna Krishna Hare Hare/ Hare Rama Hare Rama, Rama Rama Hare Hare.

***jivatma***—the living entity – the soul – who is individual, eternal, knowledgeable and blissful and who is part and parcel of God. The *jivatma* resides in the heart and gives life to the body it inhabits.

**karma**—any material action that brings a reaction that binds one to the material world. According to the law of karma, if we cause pain and suffering to other living beings, we endure pain and suffering in return.

**karma-yoga**—the path of God realization through dedicating the fruits of one's work to God.

**kirtan**—the devotional process of narrating the glories of the Supreme Personality of Godhead or singing His Holy Names, especially the maha-mantra: Hare Krishna Hare Krishna, Krishna Krishna Hare Hare/ Hare Rama Hare Rama, Rama Rama Hare Hare.

**Krishna**—God, the all-attractive Supreme Person who is the cause of all causes, the supreme controller and the supreme proprietor.

**Krishna das Kaviraj Goswami**—(1520-1616?) the author of Chaitanya Charitamrita, considered the greatest work on Sri Chaitanya's life.
**Narottam das Thakur**—a renowned spiritual master and author of many devotional songs. He appeared in the 16th century in West Bengal and was devoted to Sri Chaitanya from birth.
**Niranjana Swami**—(1952- ) a disciple of Bhaktivedanta Swami who travels worldwide teaching God consciousness.
**Paramatma**—the Supersoul, the localized aspect of God who resides in the heart of each embodied living entity.
**Queen Kunti**—the mother of Arjuna and an elevated devotee.
**Radhanatha Swami**—(1950- ) a disciple of Bhaktivedanta Swami Prabhupada, teacher of bhakti-yoga and author of *The Journey Home.*
**Sharanagati**—a spiritually-oriented rural community in British Columbia, Canada.
**Sri Chaitanya**—the Supreme Person, Krishna, who appeared as His own devotee to follow and teach the process of bhakti-yoga.
**Sri Isopanisad**—one of the 108 Upanisads, containing knowledge that brings one nearer to God.
**Srimad-Bhagavatam**—compiled by Srila Vyasadeva, the complete science of God that establishes the supreme position of Krishna.
**Supersoul**—Paramatma in Sanskrit, God who resides next to the soul in the heart of each embodied living entity. He is the living entity's witness, permitter and friend and from Him come the living entity's knowledge, remembrance and forgetfulness.
**Svetasvatara Upanisad**—one of the 108 Upanisads.
**Taittiriya Upanisad**—one of the 108 Upanisads.
**Varsana Swami**—a disciple of Bhaktivedanta Swami Prabhupada.
**Vishnu Purana**—a scripture describing the glories of God.
**Visvanath Chakravarti Thakur**—(1638?-1708?) a devout follower of Sri Chaitanya who composed valuable books on the science of bhakti.

# Acknowledgements

To my family, John, Shyam, Rasamrita, Priya and Kunja for their great company. To the residents of Sharanagati Village for being there through times both hot and cold. To Michael Cremo, Carl E. Woodham, Beth Bauer, Ortrun Gates, Marie Ann Ostlund, Anne Dooney and Kumari-priya Devi for aiding the fledgling manuscript. To the Radhadesh community in Belgium for facilitating a rewrite. To Rasikananda Das for rescuing the cover. To Lynn Edwards and Luiza Draganska for proofreading despite busy schedules. And to Donna Sugg, Yamuna Devi and Kaisori Bellach for help and perennial optimism.

# The Author

Visakha (pronounced Vish-A-khA) received an Associate of Applied Science degree with honors from Rochester Institute of Technology and shortly afterwards published her first book, *Photomacrography: Art and Techniques.* In 1971 she traveled to India, where she met Bhaktivedanta Swami Prabhupada, read his *Bhagavad-gita As It Is* and eventually became his student. As a photographer, she traveled with and photographed Bhaktivedanta Swami and his students in India, Europe and the United States. As a writer, she wrote numerous magazine articles and two books, *Our Most Dear Friend,* a Bhagavad-gita for children, and *Bhagavad-gita, A Photographic Essay,* an award-winning, fully illustrated summary study of the Bhagavad-gita. Visakha also assists her husband, John Griesser, in making documentary films. They have two daughters and are based in Sharanagati Village, a rural community in British Columbia, Canada, where Visakha is writing a memoir.

Priya

Made in the USA
Charleston, SC
09 December 2014